THOU SHALT NOT LACK!

UNDERSTANDING GOD'S PROVISION FOR YOU

JEFF MILLER

MILLER MINISTRIES

Thou Shalt Not Lack
ISBN 978-0-9846918-2-1
Copyright © 2013 by Jeffrey J. Miller
Published by Miller Ministries
P.O. Box 6404, Aurora, IL, 60598
PastorsJeffandChristine.org

First Edition: 2013

Unless otherwise indicated, all Scripture quotations are taken from the *King James Version* of the Bible.

Scripture quotations marked *AMP* are taken from the AMPLIFIED® Bible. Copyright © 1954, 1958, 1962, 1964, 1965, 1987 by The Lockman Foundation. Used by permission. (www.Lockman.org)

Scripture quotations marked *NKJV* are taken from the NEW KING JAMES VERSION®.Copyright © 1982 by Thomas Nelson, Inc. Used by permission. All rights reserved.

Scripture quotations marked *NLT* are taken from the Holy Bible, NEW LIVING TRANSLATION. Copyright © 1996, 2004, 2007 by Tyndale House Foundation. Used by permission of Tyndale House Publishers, Inc., Carol Stream, IL 60188. All rights reserved.

Scripture quotations marked *The Message* are taken from THE MESSAGE. Copyright © 1993, 1994, 1995, 1996, 2000, 2001, 2002. Used by permission of NavPress Publishing Group.

Scripture quotations marked *Phillips* are taken from J. B. Phillips, *The New Testament in Modern English*, copyright © 1962 edition, published by HarperCollins.

Scripture quotations marked TLB are taken from THE LIVING BIBLE. Copyright © 1971 by Tyndale House Publishers, Carol Stream, IL 60188. All rights reserved.

Scripture quotations marked *Weymouth's* are taken from the WEYMOUTH NEW TESTAMENT IN MODERN SPEECH, Third Edition. Copyright © 1913.

Printed in the United States of America. All rights reserved under International Copyright Law. No portion of this book and/or cover may be reproduced, stored in a retrieval system, or transmitted in any form or by any means —electronic, mechanical, photocopy, recording, or any other—except for brief quotations in printed reviews, without the prior written consent of the publisher.

Table of Contents

Endorsement 5

Dedication..7

Foreword..9

Preface 11

Chapter 1 God's View of Prosperity.........................13

Chapter 2 How Much is Too Much?..........................23

Chapter 3 Get Liberated! 33

Chapter 4 Jesus Was Not Poor 53

Chapter 5 Abraham's Blessings Are Yours 67

Chapter 6 Get Wisdom and Understanding!...........87

Chapter 7 Prosperity Has a Purpose 99

Chapter 8 Get Your Soul in Gear!...........................109

Chapter 9 Practical Principles of Prosperity.........127

Prayer for Salvation..154

About the Author 155

Endorsement

The majority of God's people are living beneath what God has provided for them. Many are unaware of all that He has made theirs, so they struggle needlessly.

Prosperity is not just about how much money someone can have; prosperity is a way of thinking—thinking in line with God's Word. The enemy will oppose us more in the financial arena than any other arena. But the Word has much to say on the subject, and from it we know that the supply God has prepared for us far surpasses any need we will ever face.

For the rest of our lives, we will need to renew our minds with the Word of God regarding prosperity. The Word will guard our hearts and minds so that we don't allow the economy, circumstances, or the wrong ways we have been raised to cause us to think incorrectly about prosperity.

The desire you have to prosper didn't originate with you, but with God. Therefore, He has richly provided all that you will ever need through Christ Jesus. I appreciate Pastor Jeff Miller for setting forth these principles on prosperity from God's Word in simplicity. His teaching undeniably shows that prosperity is God's will for all His people, and it enables them to easily grasp what God has provided.

As you faithfully do God's Word, your life will be a testimony to the timeless truth that "Thou Shalt Not Lack."

Nancy Dufresne
Murrieta, California

Dedication

I dedicate this book to my beautiful wife, Christine. You are the greatest gift I have received outside of my salvation. This book would not have been published without your help. I thank God for bringing you into my life – I love you.

Foreword

Many Christians are living a life of financial lack. Yet both the Old and New Testaments are full of promises that address financial need. Financial provision is not only a promise but a right of every born-again believer. Because of either a lack of revelation, or a lack of implementing the revelation received, Christians everywhere have suffered needlessly.

There are still misunderstandings in the church about the role of money. However, the Scriptures make it clear that it is not money that is the root of all evil, but "the love of money" that corrupts. Because of wrong thinking, much of the church has lived like those under a curse instead of living a life of blessing.

Pastor Jeff Miller has had a strong anointing to teach on the subject of prosperity since 1982, which has been recognized by many notable ministers and members of the body of Christ. His unique teachings have helped countless people to receive financial increase supernaturally. Oftentimes, people have acquired finances in spectacular ways after receiving an impartation through the laying on of hands.

This book presents Biblical truths in a powerful way, revealing God's intent to financially bless His people. To the author, it is a divine mandate to make these truths available and see Christians blessed financially. This mandate was recently confirmed by a longstanding congregation member who had an angelic visitation proclaiming that these truths be published.

As the church enters the end of the last days before Jesus returns, it is critical that provision is available to fund the harvest. It is important that Christians understand that God has given them the power to get wealth to get the Gospel out to the nations. The truths presented in this book will reveal how Christians can prosper and fund the end-time harvest. Get ready to discover the truth of what God says about prosperity!

Preface

The phrase "Thou shalt not" occurs 240 times in the King James Version of the Bible. Most people are familiar with "thou shalt not kill," "thou shalt not commit adultery," "thou shalt not steal," "thou shalt not covet," "thou shalt not bear false witness," and the other commandments. However, few have ever contemplated "thou shalt not lack." One day while reading the book of Deuteronomy, the phrase "**Thou shalt not lack**" jumped out at me. The Scripture says,

> **DEUTERONOMY 8:7-10**
> 7 For the Lord thy God bringeth thee into a good land, a land of brooks of water, of fountains and depths that spring out of valleys and hills;
> 8 A land of wheat, and barley, and vines, and fig trees, and pomegranates; a land of oil olive, and honey;
> 9 A land wherein thou shalt eat bread without scarceness, **THOU SHALT NOT LACK** any thing in it; a land whose stones are iron, and out of whose hills thou mayest dig brass.
> 10 When thou hast eaten and art full, then thou shalt bless the Lord thy God for the good land which he hath given thee.

As I spent some time meditating on the phrase "thou shalt not lack," I became so blessed I ended up preaching a series of messages on the subject. This book is a result of that initial inspiration.

Just as much as God is against killing, stealing, fornicating, and lying (to name a few), He is also against His people living in lack. If under the Old Covenant God's people were not to lack anything, how could we, living under the New and better Covenant, have anything less? Does the Creator of the universe desire His children to suffer want? I believe the Scriptures clearly teach that God's people should live a life free from lack of any good thing. If we have given our lives to Jesus Christ, and are actively serving him, His desire is to bring us to a place of total provision.

CHAPTER 1

God's View of Prosperity

The topic of prosperity is very controversial in the church of the Lord Jesus Christ and has been labeled many things by critics. It has been called "the faith message," "the prosperity gospel," "the name it and claim it gospel," "the blab it and grab it gospel," "the health and wealth gospel," and "the hyper-faith movement." This subject gets more people riled up than almost anything.

Even many who embrace the message of healing have difficulty believing that God wants His people prosperous. There are so many false doctrines in the church world and plenty of excesses that would lend themselves to criticism. But much of the criticism of prosperity is the result of an unrenewed mind—a mind that has not seen the clear picture of what the Bible teaches about this subject.

Scripture plainly teaches that Jesus came to save the lost. It also clearly declares that healing and prosperity are included in His substitutionary work. The Word of God says,

JOHN 10:10
10 The thief cometh not, but for to steal, and to kill, and to destroy: I am come that they might have life, and that they might have it more ABUNDANTLY.

This is one of the scriptures that many Christians like to allocate as meaning only "spiritual" abundance. But the full meaning of this verse is having abundance in *all* areas of one's life. Many other scriptures confirm this, such as this one in 3 John:

3 JOHN 2 *(NKJV)*
2 Beloved, I pray that you may PROSPER in all things and be in health, just as your soul PROSPERS.

Other translations use the words "desire" and "wish above all else" in place of the word "pray." Clearly, this is not just a passing greeting. This is the prayer of the beloved apostle of Jesus Christ, John. Remember, John wrote this by inspiration of the Holy Spirit, so *prospering in all things* is the desire of the Lord Himself.

Three Key Verses to Know

God wants His church to come into agreement with what His Word says, not with what the world says! Therefore, we must rightly divide (accurately handle) His Word on the subject of prosperity. Here are three passages worth taking note of regarding this subject:

PSALM 1:1-3
1 Blessed is the man that walketh not in the counsel of the ungodly, nor standeth in the way of sinners, nor sitteth in the seat of the scornful.

2 But his delight is in the law of the Lord; and in his law doth he meditate day and night.
3 And he shall be like a tree planted by the rivers of water, that bringeth forth his fruit in his season; his leaf also shall not wither; and whatsoever he doeth shall prosper.

JOSHUA 1:8
8 This book of the law shall not depart out of thy mouth; but thou shalt meditate therein day and night, that thou mayest observe to do according to all that is written therein: for then thou shalt make thy way prosperous, and then thou shalt have good success.

ISAIAH 1:19
19 If ye be willing and obedient, ye shall eat the good of the land.

All of these verses teach us how to prosper: by reading and meditating on the Word of God daily and obeying it. If God didn't want us to *prosper*, if He didn't want us to *have good success*, and if He didn't want us to *eat the good of the land*, why would He tell us how to do just that?

God wants His church to agree with what His Word says, not with what the world says!

Job Was Abundantly Blessed

In order to get a good idea of God's view of prosperity, let's take a look at the life of Job. Can anything good come out of Job? Yes, I believe it can! The book of Job was written before the book of Genesis and is believed to be the oldest book in the Bible. It reveals the plan of God from very early on in the history of man. It says,

> **JOB 1:1-3 *(NKJV)***
> **1 There was a man in the land of Uz, whose name was Job; and that man was blameless and upright, and one who feared God and shunned evil.**
> **2 And seven sons and three daughters were born to him.**
> **3 Also, his possessions were seven thousand sheep, three thousand camels, five hundred yoke of oxen, five hundred female donkeys, and a very large household, so that this man was the greatest of all the people of the East.**

In Job's day, livestock and land were a large part of the people's wealth. Job had 7,000 sheep! I have one dog and an acre of land. I cannot imagine owning 7,000 sheep. One thing is for sure, an acre of land is not enough to handle 7,000 sheep!

One source cites that, on average, one acre of land is needed for every ten sheep. That would mean 700 acres of land would be needed to care for Job's sheep. That's not factoring in the camels, oxen, and donkeys!

Job had 3,000 camels! Research indicates that roughly two acres are needed per camel to care for them properly. Therefore, 3,000 camels require about 6,000 acres of land.

Job also had 500 yoke of oxen. A yoke is a pair, so that means he had 1,000 oxen. It takes about 5.75 acres of land to sustain *one* ox. Therefore, 500 yoke of oxen require 5,750 acres of land.

Let's not forget, Job also had 500 female donkeys. Generally, it takes 1 acre of land to sustain one horse or donkey. So he would have needed an additional 500 acres of land to care for 500 donkeys.

When you add up all the land Job needed to care for his 12,500 animals, it comes to a total of 12,950 acres. Wow! Can you imagine all the manure that many animals produced?

Now if Job had 500 yoke of oxen, he must have also had *extra* land for farming. To handle these 500 yoke of oxen, he would have needed about 500 servants. Two or three hired hands just wouldn't have been enough to get the job done.

The Scripture confirms that Job had "a very large household." Not only did he have a wife and ten children, he undoubtedly had multitudes of servants to take care of his possessions. Indeed, Job was the greatest man of all the people of the East.

Now some might say, "Who needs all those animals and all those acres of land? Isn't that a little wasteful? Isn't that a little extravagant? Wouldn't a flock of 100 be prosperous enough? Why would Job need 7,000 sheep?"

Should we assume that Job was a sinner since he was so blessed with material possessions? No, absolutely not! We just read that Job was "blameless and upright, one who feared God and shunned evil" (Job 1:1).

After the Test, Job Was Doubly Blessed

We know from Scripture what happened to Job. Satan smote him and he lost everything he had except his wife. Many people who are going through difficult times compare themselves to "good old Job." The next time someone tells you, "I'm just like good old Job," you should respond by saying, "Praise the Lord!" That is likely to shock them, but the truth is Job's end was far greater than his beginning. The Scripture says,

> **JOB 42:10** *(NKJV)*
> **10 And the Lord restored Job's losses when he prayed for his friends. Indeed the Lord gave Job *twice as much* as he had before.**

Notice it doesn't say the devil restored Job's losses, nor does it say that Job's friends restored his losses or that Job did it himself. It says "The Lord restored Job's losses." This means that God didn't mind him having all that wealth! Two verses later we read,

> **JOB 42:12** *(NKJV)*
> **12 Now the Lord blessed the latter days of Job more than his beginning; for he had fourteen thousand sheep, six thousand camels, one thousand yoke of oxen, and one thousand female donkeys.**

In the end, Job had a total of 23,000 farm animals. These required twice as much land as he had originally. Do the math and you'll discover he needed 25,900 acres of land just to care for his animals.

The Lord restored Job's losses. Obviously, God didn't think Job's wealth was excessive.

What else did God bless him with?

JOB 42:13
13 He also had seven sons and three daughters.

How did Job finish his life?

JOB 42:17
17 So Job died, being old and full of days.

Bible scholars agree that Job's difficulty lasted only nine to twelve months. He was clearly under attack from the devil. But God turned it around and gave him twice as much as he had before!

God Doesn't Think the Way We Think

I'm sure there were plenty of people in Job's day who didn't have one acre of land or even one farm animal. Did Job need all of those possessions when there were people in the land who had nothing? Why did one man who had ten children need 23,000 farm animals? If each of his children had ten animals, that would be 100 animals. Wouldn't that be enough? Worldly thinking says, "Spread those animals around! Give some to those who don't have any!" Even some believers might question, "Are you sure this isn't excessive, God?"

Obviously God didn't think it was excessive! There are plenty of people today who think that abundance, especially in the life of a preacher or a Christian, is excessive. But God's view is different than man's view. He says,

ISAIAH 55:8-9
8 For my thoughts are not your thoughts, neither are your ways my ways, saith the Lord.

9 For as the heavens are higher than the earth, so are my ways higher than your ways, and my thoughts than your thoughts.

Can you imagine what people would think if a pastor with a church of 100 members had 25,900 acres of land to house his 23,000 farm animals? They would think he was selling drugs, in the mafia, or stealing money from somewhere.

Most people cannot understand how faith in God's Word can make a person prosperous. The natural mind automatically assumes that something dishonest is taking place if a Christian is very blessed financially. This is why it is so important to learn God's view of prosperity.

Let's establish this truth once again: It was the LORD who restored Job's losses. The LORD gave him twice as much as he had before his trials, and this was prior to the covenant He had made with Abraham. The Scripture says,

JOB 42:16-17
16 After this lived Job an hundred and forty years, and saw his sons, and his sons' sons, even four generations.
17 So Job died, being old and full of days.

After all the blessing, the calamity, and then double blessing, Job lived another 140 years. When he died, he was *full of days*, which means "satisfied." **That is God's view of prosperity!**

Are you beginning to see and understand God's desire to bless His people? He loves you and wants you to prosper and be in health and represent Him well on the earth. Yes, you may experience times of trial and seasons of need, but as you hold onto God's promises and trust Him to keep His Word, He will turn the tide and be glorified in your life!

Chapter 1 Summary

God desires to bring you, His child, to a place of total provision. Jesus came that you might have an abundant life. He wants you to prosper in all things, not just spiritually. As you feed on His Word and obey it, you will enjoy the good of the land. Just as God abundantly blessed Job, He desires to abundantly bless you. Yes, you will go through tests and trials, but in the end you will be doubly blessed as you trust in His Word and refuse to conform to the thinking of the world.

CHAPTER 2

How Much Is Too Much?

When it comes to the story of Job, many will say, "That was then, this is now." But God declares in Malachi 3:6, "I am the Lord, I change not," and in Psalm 35:27, He says He has "...pleasure in the prosperity of His servant."

Many will concede that God wants His children blessed, but they have difficulty believing that God would want them to be blessed *abundantly*. This brings us to an important question: **How much is too much?**

Are 23,000 animals too much? What would someone do with 6,000 camels anyway? In ancient times, camels were used for transportation, military combat, milk, and meat. Under Jewish dietary laws, camels are not considered kosher because they do not have cloven hooves. However, Job lived before the dietary laws were given, so it is very likely that the camels were used both for milk and food in his household. These are just some of the possibilities.

Comparatively speaking, can you imagine owning 6,000 horses or cars? I am just trying to expand your thinking to see that our view and God's view are not the same. As a matter of fact, the view of prosperity even differs from person to person.

Each Person's View of Prosperity Is Subjective

Now you may be thinking, *This doesn't apply to me. I'm just trying to obtain one car. I'm just trying to find a place to live. I'm just trying to provide food for my family.* The truth is, it *does* apply to you and here's why: Until you get God's view of your situations, your perception and thinking will be wrong, and it will keep you living on a considerably lower level.

Some people think that God doesn't necessarily want them poor, but He does want them to live a "normal" life. Well, what's a "normal" life? When it comes to finances, how is "normal" defined? Every person's view is relative to where they are financially. If someone earns $100,000 per year, then earning $120,000 a year would not seem like a lot. But if someone only earns $25,000 per year, then earning $120,000 would probably seem like a huge amount.

From a business perspective, if a business earned $10,000 per week, which is $520,000 a year, it would *not* be considered a large business. It would be considered a small one. Even a business earning $1 million dollars a year is not considered a large company. However, an average individual could compare his personal income to this amount and think it is huge. Of course, for someone like Oprah Winfrey, $1 million a year is chump change. But compared to what God has, this is nothing!

Measured against Him, we are all dirt poor! He lives on streets paved with pure gold!

So each person's view of prosperity is subjective. That's why we need God's view. His perspective is unchanging. God's view is the solid foundation upon which we can base our beliefs about prosperity.

God's view is the solid foundation upon which we can base our beliefs about prosperity.

The Old Covenant vs. the New Covenant

Before Christ came and established the New Covenant with all who would believe in Him, all followers of God were connected with Him through the Old Covenant of the Law. In it, God says,

> DEUTERONOMY 8:1
> 1 All the commandments which I command thee this day shall ye observe to do, that ye may live, and MULTIPLY, and go in and possess the land which the Lord sware unto your fathers.

> DEUTERONOMY 8:7-10
> 7 For the Lord thy God bringeth thee into a good land, a land of brooks of water, of fountains and depths that spring out of valleys and hills;
> 8 A land of wheat, and barley, and vines, and fig trees, and pomegranates; a land of oil olive, and honey;
> 9 A land wherein thou shalt eat bread without scarceness, THOU SHALT NOT LACK ANY THING

in it; a land whose stones are iron, and out of whose hills thou mayest dig brass.

10 When thou hast eaten and art full, then thou shalt bless the Lord thy God for the good land which he hath given thee.

Under the Old Covenant, God provided His people with abundantly fertile land that was well watered. The produce it yielded was diverse and abundant, and even the rocks were chock-full of valuable ores. Without question, God's people did not lack any good thing.

Today, Jesus Christ is the "...Mediator of a better covenant, which was established on better promises" (Hebrews 8:6 NKJV). So if God abundantly blessed those who obeyed Him under the Old Covenant, how much more will He bless us who obey Him under the New Covenant? How could we have less under a *better* covenant?

God's idea of just a little bit more is no less than *double*. We can see this in the examples of Job and the parable of the talents (see Matthew 25:14-22). The minimum whole number multiplier is 2, because any number multiplied by 1 stays the same. Therefore, doubling is the minimum multiple of increase.

Make It Personal

Now let's personalize God's promises in Deuteronomy 8 and read it like He is speaking directly to us:

"I, the Lord, am bringing YOU into a good land, a land with brooks of water."
—Deuteronomy 8:7, author's paraphrase

You may be thinking, *I would just be happy to have a piece of property with a street in front of it.* But why don't you start imagining a piece of property with a stream, a creek, or a brook on it? Wouldn't that be nice?

The Lord continues...

"I am bringing YOU into a land where you will eat bread without scarceness, and YOU SHALL NOT LACK anything in it! And when you have eaten and are full, then you shall bless the Lord your God for the good land which HE has given you."
—Deuteronomy 8:9-10, author's paraphrase

Now, hear the warning God gives to you and all others He knows will be blessed:

DEUTERONOMY 8:11-14
11 Beware that thou forget not the Lord thy God, in not keeping his commandments, and his judgments, and his statutes, which I command thee this day:
12 Lest when thou hast eaten and art full, and hast built goodly houses, and dwelt therein;
13 And when thy herds and thy flocks multiply, and thy silver and thy gold is multiplied, and all that thou hast is multiplied;
14 Then thine heart be lifted up, and thou forget the Lord thy God....

There are those who will serve God when they have nothing and then depart from serving Him after they become wealthy. Having wealth is not the root of the problem. The wealth simply reveals what is in a person's heart—a loyalty and devotion to God, or to money and material gain. If the blessings are what make a person turn away from God, then why would He bless His people?

There are also people who stop thanking and praising God for their blessings once they receive them. They become lifted up in pride, thinking they have done such great things in their own strength and ability to obtain their wealth. Nothing could be farther from the truth. Enjoy the blessings God gives and never forget about Him! Keep His commandments and thank Him for His goodness.

My spiritual father is a very blessed man. Some people have looked at his prosperity and misjudged his motives. What they do not know or have overlooked is the fact that he was willing to obey God without pay early on in his Christian walk. He quit his paying job to build a church for his pastor without receiving any pay. He had to believe God to supply his needs for over a year. Many Christians would not obey God to that extent, which is why they aren't as financially blessed. Obedience opens the door for God to bless us on every level. My spiritual father experienced this. He proved early on that he wasn't serving God for money. Consequently, God honored His Word and made sure that he was blessed with plenty for his willingness and obedience. As He promised through the prophet Isaiah,

ISAIAH 1:19
19 If ye be willing and *obedient*, ye shall eat the good of the land.

My Motivation for Preaching

Some have thought that I was preaching prosperity just for the money. The fact is, I started preaching prosperity when I was only earning $50 a week in full-time ministry! I had finished one year of college and graduated from two Bible schools. And my "huge" salary at the age of 25 was $50 a week, without benefits.

I didn't go into the ministry for money. But my willingness and obedience to God's instructions for my life over the years have brought me financial prosperity. Being in the ministry does not guarantee prosperity. I know plenty of ministers who are not prospering. Obedience to God's Spirit and His Word guarantees provision. It's for everyone, not just preachers!

Many thought I was too religious and should have chosen a career that would pay better. Well-meaning family and friends said I had made a serious error in my career choice because of my low income when I began. But then, after I started prospering, some of the same people became critical about the increase. This taught me a powerful principle early on: I will never be able to please everyone around me and God at the same time. The things of the Spirit, including God's view of prosperity, cannot be understood by the natural mind. As the Scripture says,

1 CORINTHIANS 2:14
14 But the natural man receiveth not the things of the Spirit of God: for they are foolishness unto him: neither can he know them, because they are spiritually discerned.

The world doesn't like it when God's people prosper. They don't mind it when a professional athlete gets rich. If he purchases a $300,000 Ferrari or a multi-million dollar house, it's no big deal. But if a preacher were to buy a car or house of that value, it would make headlines!

**Obedience to God's Spirit
and His Word guarantees provision.
It's for everyone, not just preachers!**

We have to cleanse ourselves from the world's thinking, especially the messages delivered by the media. If you watch the news a lot, I suggest you double up on reading God's Word! We are always to measure our lives by Scripture, not by the thoughts of men who are governed by money.

Many in the church world have stated that God promises to supply our needs, but He never promised to provide our desires or wants. But they have overlooked this verse:

PSALM 37:4
4 Delight thyself also in the Lord; and he shall give thee the *desires* of thine heart.

With the world's way of thinking, we cannot explain Job having 23,000 animals. But with God's way of thinking, Job's abundance makes total sense. He is *El Shaddai*—the Almighty, All-Sufficient One! He is *Jehovah Jireh*, the Lord our Provider! Having too much is not an issue with Him as long as He has our hearts' humble devotion.

We have just scratched the surface of God's view of financial prosperity. He wants us to start thinking like Him. And as we do, His prosperity will break through in every area of our lives!

Chapter 2 Summary

Each person's view of prosperity is subjective and relative to where they are financially. That's why we need God's view. It's unchanging and enables us to yield the most lucrative dividends ever imagined. Until you get God's view of your situations, your perspective and thinking will be wrong, and it will keep you living on a considerably lower level. Enjoy the blessings God gives and never forget about Him! Keep His commandments and thank Him for His goodness. Obedience to His Holy Spirit and His Word guarantees provision. It's for everyone, not just preachers!

Chapter 3

Get Liberated!

You cannot believe everything you hear because it isn't always true. The news continually reminds us that we are living in difficult economic times. Yet, just a few years ago, the amount of people in the U.S. who had a net worth of more than $1 million increased 16 percent. I bring this to your attention for one purpose: When you hear someone say, "Everybody's struggling financially," it isn't true! Don't believe it.

Last year, my wife and I had the greatest year financially ever. And more than half of all our income came from sources *outside* of our salary and our local church. My point: Don't limit yourself to your job for your income. Get liberated! Expand the borders of your expectations! Even if you have never earned or received one penny from outside of your salary, don't limit God by your past experiences. Your experiences should not determine your belief system. There is a higher, more superior source of thinking. That source is the truth of God's Word!

God's Truth Trumps Everything!

In the Bible, there was a man named Isaac who sowed seed during a time of famine. Most people do not sow during a famine. But Isaac did, and he reaped one hundred times what he sowed! Perhaps if the weather had been good, he would have reaped even more. But to reap anything during a famine is reason to rejoice! Why did Isaac reap? Because he obeyed God's Word, supernatural blessings were released into his life.

During difficult economic times, the people who prosper are those who do what most people will not do: They sow seed where God tells them. While the majority is moved by a belief system of fear, prosperous people freely give and invest where God directs. The voice of fear says, "Hang on to your seed. You may need it for food. You may need it to sow next year's crop. It's not wise to plant during a time of famine." In the natural, the chances of someone experiencing lack during a famine are greater than ever before. But God's Word trumps the world's fear-driven system. He says,

> **JEREMIAH 17:7-8**
> 7 Blessed is the man that trusteth in the Lord, and whose hope the Lord is.
> 8 For he shall be as a tree planted by the waters, and that spreadeth out her roots by the river, and shall not see when heat cometh, but her leaf shall be green; and shall not be careful in the year of drought, neither shall cease from yielding fruit.

My mother was born in 1929 and raised in a family of seven children. It was the end of the Roaring Twenties, and the Great Depression was setting in. Her family was very poor. During that same year, my father was seven years old. He vividly remembers seeing men on the streets with signs asking to work from sunrise to sunset just to provide a meal for their families. The Great Depression made an indelible mark on the minds of that generation in the area of money. Some of us were raised by that generation and have felt the impact of that thinking all our lives.

Amazingly, in the midst of all the lack that many people suffered during the Great Depression, there were people who managed to build great empires and obtain great wealth. Their formula for success was to do something different, not what everyone had always done. There is always a way to prosper, regardless of economic times and seasons. God knows how and He will reveal it to those who seek Him. Through Isaiah, He said:

> **ISAIAH 48:17 *(NKJV)***
> **17 Thus says the Lord, your Redeemer, The Holy One of Israel: "I am the Lord your God, Who teaches you to profit, Who leads you by the way you should go.**

Get Rid of Wrong Thinking

God has a way for His people to prosper, but in order to do so, we need to identify and get rid of any "sacred cows," or wrong thinking that we have. There is a lot of tradition in the church world, but if tradition is not based on truth, it makes the Word of God of no effect, and we need to get rid of it.

Fear rules many people's financial decisions. There are many who are in a financial position to upgrade their level of living, but they won't do it because they are afraid of what the future may bring. There are others who God is calling to start a business of their own, but fear of failure is hindering them from obeying. There are still others who should be giving generously to their churches, but fear is causing them to withhold their financial contributions. By doing so, they are missing out on an even bigger blessing.

It's been said that FEAR is *False Evidence Appearing Real*, and this saying holds true in regards to finances. Here are three common misconceptions that hinder people from experiencing the abundant life Jesus died to provide:

#1: "It Takes Money to Make Money."

"It takes money to make money." How many times have I heard that? Others have said it this way: "If I only had $10,000, then I could really do something with it." There is no question that if you have some money, you have seed to work with. But where in the Bible does God say, "It takes *money* to make money?" Nowhere! This is a false statement that has appeared real.

The truth is, it takes **seed** to get a harvest. So the question you need to ask yourself is, *What seed do I have?* Your seed may not be in the form of money. But whatever God has placed in your hand, He will use as seed to bring a harvest in your life. God's way of prospering us is not by providing some big windfall to save us from years of poor decisions. Yes, He can do big things, but if that's all we're looking for, we will miss out on many opportunities to sow the seed we have and be blessed as a result.

God can do big things, but if that's all you're looking for, you'll miss out on many opportunities to sow the seed you have and be blessed.

#2: "The Lottery…That's the Ticket!"

When you fall behind and come under financial pressure, you may be very tempted to do something that looks like it's going to provide a quick payoff. I'm talking about the trap of gambling. I don't believe in it and never will. I have never purchased a lottery ticket or spent $1 on it. Some people may think, *Can't you afford a dollar?* Yes, I can, but I also know how to use a calculator.

The odds of you or me winning the lottery in any given state average about 18 million to 1. The odds are actually greater for us to be struck by lightning than to win the lottery.[1] Don't buy the lie that the lottery is your ticket to prosperity. It's not, and you should never spend a dollar on it.

I stayed in a casino hotel once, and the reason I did was because it was a host hotel for the conference I attended. The rooms were very nice and came at a great price. During my stay, I remember getting on the elevator to go up to my room, and there were a few depressed, drunk people riding with me. I looked at them and asked, "How much did you make?"

"Not a thing," they responded as they hung their heads in despair.

I said, "I've been here all week, and I haven't lost a penny!" That got their attention. They looked at me in total astonishment. After a few minutes of letting them wonder, I said, "I don't gamble."

"You're smart!" they replied. Too bad they didn't meet me before they started gambling. I could have saved them some money and helped them avoid some misery. Again, don't buy the lie that the lottery or gambling of any kind is your ticket to prosperity. It's not. Trusting and obeying God's Word is. Remember,

> **PROVERBS 28:20** *(THE MESSAGE)*
> **20 Committed and persistent work pays off; get-rich-quick schemes are ripoffs.**

#3: "But *What If* Something Terrible Happens?"

In this life, there is a healthy, natural reverence or respect for the laws of life. Like the respect for the power of electricity that keeps us from touching high voltage wires and the healthy fear of fire that keeps us from sticking our hands on a red hot stove.

I'm not a fearful man, but I do have a healthy reverence for the law of gravity. It keeps me from walking a tight rope between two skyscrapers or from hanging over a cliff while sightseeing. That queasy feeling you get when you are too close to the edge means "don't go any further." This kind of reverential fear is healthy and life-preserving.

There are many other fears, however, that are totally unfounded. They are based on countless "what ifs" in life. "*What if* I lose my job? *What if* I get into an accident and crash my car? *What if* I lose all my money in an investment?" Our church is close to two major Chicago airports. "*What if* one of the thousands of airplanes that fly over us crashes into our building during a church service?" A person who always thinks about the *what ifs* will be a fearful scatterbrain, void of peace and unable to enjoy his life.

On the other hand, a person with a healthy, sound mind is not going to focus on *what ifs*. The possibility of plane crashes, car crashes, and stock market crashes are not going to rule their thinking. God's Word will. If you have been tossed to and fro by the *what ifs* of life, seek the presence of God. Allow the truth of His Word, which promises a prosperous, abundant life, to liberate you. As you spend time with Him and meditate on Truth, He will change your fear-based thinking to faith-based thinking.

Meditating on the Word Produces Prosperity

Without question, meditating on the Word of God produces prosperous thinking. Meditation is not just an activity associated with eastern religions. It is actually a God-approved practice that He repeatedly instructs us to do in Scripture. He says,

> **JOSHUA 1:8**
> 8 This book of the law shall not depart out of thy mouth; but thou shalt *meditate* therein day and night, that thou mayest observe to do according to all that is written therein: for then thou shalt make thy way prosperous, and then thou shalt have good success.
>
> **PSALM 1:1-3**
> 1 Blessed is the man that walketh not in the counsel of the ungodly, nor standeth in the way of sinners, nor sitteth in the seat of the scornful.
> 2 But his delight is in the law of the Lord; and in his law doth he *meditate* day and night.
> 3 And he shall be like a tree planted by the rivers of water, that bringeth forth his fruit in his season; his leaf also shall not wither; and whatsoever he doeth shall prosper.

Meditating on the Word day and night is a recipe for true prosperity. What does it mean to *meditate*? It simply means "to mutter under your breath" or "speak something softly to yourself over and over." If you know how to worry, you know how to meditate. Instead of rolling a problem over and over in your mind, roll God's promises. Say them softly to yourself again and again, and they will become an integral part of your thinking, speaking, and acting.

Now, you may not believe this, but I'm going to say it anyway. If you are going to be a Christian and serve God and receive His blessings in your life, it is going to come by meditating on the Word. The Word is your answer, not winning the lottery or having a rich relative leave you an inheritance.

God, through His Word and the guidance of His Spirit, will show you how to use the talent, ability, resources, and skills you currently have to get to the next level without going deeper into debt. You may not become rich or debt-free over night, but little by little, true prosperity will permeate every area of your life. As you act wisely at one level, He will take you to the next.

You could be fifteen years old now, and by the time you reach twenty, you could be making $100,000 a year. How? By meditating on God's Word and following the Holy Spirit's leading. He will empower you to operate with a standard of excellence just as Daniel did in days of old (see Daniel 5:11-12).

This is the land of opportunity, and God knows how to prosper you. But you will only hear His voice guiding you if you are spending time with Him. So give your attention to meditating on His Word and following the direction of the Holy Spirit. Quality time with the Lord each day is a priceless investment that pays off big time!

True Enjoyment of Prosperity Can Only Come to Christians

Rich people who are not trusting in God will always have a degree of fear regarding their money. I personally believe that only Christians who are truly committed to serving God can enjoy wealth. As some have said, the blessing of the Lord is *sorrow-free* money. The Lord confirms this through King Solomon:

> **PROVERBS 10:22**
> **22 The blessing of the Lord, it maketh rich, and *he addeth no sorrow with it.***

Wealth itself is *not* what makes a person happy. An unbeliever may be happy temporarily with possessions, vacations, and money. But true contentment is not based on anything external. It is based on the *eternal* condition of a person's soul and spirit. Jesus said,

> **MATTHEW 16:26**
> **26 For what is a man profited, if he shall gain the whole world, and lose his own soul?**

The spiritual or eternal part of man is worth far more than anything of this earth. If a person has wealth, but does not have eternal life, he will still be miserable.

If you think about it, there are only two families in this world: the family of God and the family of Satan. Whether people know it or not, they are in one or the other. There is a saying that goes along with this: "There are three types of people in the world; thems that is, thems that ain't, and thems that ain't but thinks they is." I know that's not great English, so let me clarify. Basically this means, *Many people think they belong to God, but they don't.*

A well-known preacher used to be one of those who thought he was a Christian, but was not. As a seventeen-year-old boy, he was overcome by an incurable disease. He actually died and was on his way to hell.

During that experience, he cried out to God, saying, "Lord, I'm going the wrong way! I'm a member of the church." But the Lord revealed to him that just being a church member isn't enough to get a person into heaven. We must repent of our sins and surrender our lives to Jesus in order to be saved and become part of God's family.

The family you are in determines whether or not you have the ability to truly enjoy abundant life. Only those who are believers and belong to God's family have the potential for sorrow-free prosperity.

God Prospers Us from the Inside Out

Prosperity is a balanced life in which we are healthy spiritually, physically, mentally, emotionally, and financially. Freedom from fear is a part of godly prosperity. Again, let's look at God's Word in 3 John 2:

> **3 JOHN 2**
> **2 Beloved, I wish above all things that thou mayest prosper and be in health, even as thy soul prospereth.**

God's way of prospering us is always *from the inside out*. If we try to prosper from the outside in, it won't work. People who have won the lottery are a good example of this. Most were not a millionaire on the *inside* before they won. That means they were not a millionaire in their thinking or in the way they conducted their lives. As a result, winning a boatload of money ended up ruining them. This is confirmed by God in Scripture:

PROVERBS 1:32
32 The prosperity of fools shall destroy them.

PROVERBS 13:11 *(AMP)*
11 Wealth [not earned but] won in haste or unjustly or from the production of things for vain or detrimental use [such riches] will dwindle away, but he who gathers little by little will increase [his riches].

Most people are not spiritually, mentally, or emotionally ready to handle a million dollars. So if by some chance they inherit or win it, it ends up causing all kinds of trouble for them. This is also why most people do *not* receive a large windfall from God to fix their financial problems.

God's way of prospering us is always from the inside out. If we try to prosper from the outside in, it won't work.

The Lord knows what size blessing each person is able to handle. He never wants us to be destroyed by what we receive. He is in the blessing business, not the destruction business. It may be hard for us to admit that we might not be ready to handle a lot of money. Nevertheless, we must be honest with ourselves and God and come to grips with where we are in order to get to where we want to be.

How do we become prosperous? By focusing on prospering our soul. God wants us to prosper *even as* our soul prospers. The words *even as* mean "in the same way as" or "in equal proportion to." Your soul needs to expand so that you can handle a new capacity of prosperity. If you will spend your time and energy on prospering your soul—renewing your mind, will, and emotions with the Word of God—you will eventually be able to handle great increase.

God is not against Christians having wealth; He is against wealth having Christians! He is not against people who have money; He is against people who *trust* in money. Realize "the *love* of money is the root of all evil," not money itself (1 Timothy 6:10). God wants you and me to prosper and be in health to the same degree our soul prospers. As you mature and delight yourself in Him, He will prosper you and make you a blessing to others!

You Are Blessed to *Be* a Blessing

One of the main reasons for financial prosperity from the Lord is so that you can *be a blessing* to others. Few people's lives reflect this more clearly than Abraham's. When God spoke to him in Haran after his father, Terah, died, He said something very important:

GENESIS 12:2
2 And I will make of thee a great nation, and I will bless thee, and make thy name great; and thou shalt *be a blessing*.

Did you catch that? God said, "I will bless thee...and thou shalt *be a blessing*." Abraham was blessed to be a blessing, and so are we. If you are not being a blessing with what you currently have, you won't be a blessing with more.

Perhaps you are familiar with the owner of Hobby Lobby, David Green. He is a born-again Christian who has experienced great success in business. One of the reasons he is so successful is because he honors the Lord with his money and his life. He has proven through his actions that he can be trusted by God to handle his wealth in a righteous manner. He is an honorable man.

How does Mr. Green do it? First of all, Hobby Lobby is closed on Sundays. This gives his employees an opportunity to honor the Lord by resting and attending church. Secondly, he gives away millions of dollars to God-centered organizations, including money to help pay off countless church buildings. He is clearly not motivated by the fear of running out of resources. His goal is to help his pastor's vision come to pass, and he puts his time and money behind it. Amazingly, he still finds time to teach a Sunday school class. He is flowing in the purpose of his prosperity, and God will continue to bless him with more.

Are you bound by fear of lack? God can bring you out of that bondage and into prosperity! All it requires is a willing, obedient heart that is surrendered to Him. He promises,

> **JOB 36:11**
> **11 If they obey and serve him, they shall spend their days in prosperity, and their years in pleasures.**
>
> **ISAIAH 1:19**
> **19 If ye be willing and obedient, ye shall eat the good of the land:**

PSALM 68:6 *(NKJV)*
6 God sets the solitary in families; He brings out those who are bound into prosperity; But the rebellious dwell in a dry land.

Christianity shouldn't be that we give our life to Jesus, and then we go broke financially, get sick, and live miserable lives. That's Satan's desire, not God's. God desires that we experience His abundant life through Christ.

As a pastor, my vision for our church is that when people come, if they are not saved, they get saved and receive eternal life. Then, I pray that they daily renew their mind with God's Word, so they can begin to think right and experience God's peace. In Christ, they can truly enjoy their life and begin to prosper, increase, and *be a blessing* to others. If they have been sick, they can begin to get stronger and healthier. All this and more is what Jesus provided!

Stay in Your Gift

What else is important to experiencing prosperity? Finding out how God has gifted you and learning to flow in those gifts. Believe it or not, God is not up in heaven rolling the dice to determine whose lucky day it is for prosperity. There is always a cause for blessing or a reason for not being blessed, and the fault is never on God's side. Sometimes the reason for not experiencing prosperity is because we are not serving and working within our God-given gift.

Everybody has a gift, skill, or aptitude in which they can excel. The Bible says,

> **1 CORINTHIANS 12:7** *(The Message)*
> 7 Each person is given something to do that shows who God is: Everyone gets in on it, everyone benefits.

> **1 PETER 4:10** *(AMP)*
> 10 As each of you has received a gift (a particular spiritual talent, a gracious divine endowment), employ it for one another as [befits] good trustees of God's many-sided grace....

Sometimes the reason for financial failure is that we are working a job that is *not* compatible with our gifting. In this case, all the classes and coaching in the world won't make us successful. Why? Because we are not gifted to work in that area. For example, if a person aspires to have a singing career, he better have an exceptional voice. If he has a terrible singing voice and he is endeavoring to sing for a living, he has made a bad career choice.

As parents, we are to help our children discover their God-given gifts and then help develop them. We are instructed by the Lord in Proverbs to…

> **PROVERBS 22:6**
> 6 Train up a child in the way he should go: and when he is old, he will not depart from it.

The Amplified translation makes this truth even clearer:

PROVERBS 22:6 *(AMP)*
6 Train up a child in the way he should go [and in keeping with his individual *gift* or *bent*], and when he is old he will not depart from it.

Every child has an individual gift or bent—a specific way God has shaped him and a direction in which He has pointed him. As parents, we are *not* to force the bent we want our child to have. We are to pray and discover each of our children's unique God-given gifts and then help to develop those gifts in them.

Prosperity will come as we stay in our gift and serve in the way God has shaped us. If you are in your gift, you will be doing something you enjoy and are good at. Now, some people enjoy sitting on a hammock, sipping lemonade, and watching television. If that describes you, realize that kind of activity will not earn you a living or bring you into prosperity.

If you are unsure about how God has gifted you, take time to seek Him in prayer. Ask Him to show you how you are bent (and how your kids are bent too). When in doubt, step out and try something you feel you might enjoy and be good at. If it becomes a struggle and doesn't bring you inner peace and joy, step back and regroup. Your pastor will also help you to identify what gifting you have. The Lord will direct your path as you trust in Him. He will lead you into the call on your life and empower you to prosper in it.

To God, Prosperity Is a Done Deal

From God's perspective, prosperity is an accomplished fact, a done deal! Therefore, whether a person becomes prosperous or not is really a matter of individual choice. God says,

> **DEUTERONOMY 30:19**
> **19 I call heaven and earth to record this day against you, that I have set before you life and death, blessing and cursing: therefore choose life, that both thou and thy seed may live:**

The choice is clear! Choosing things that lead to life puts you on the path to prosperity. If you want blessings from God, you have to do things God's way. God's way is not working three jobs, never seeing your family, missing church, and being exhausted just to get ahead financially. That is never the will of God! Extra jobs may be His will for a season, but those jobs should never keep you from serving Him and spending time with Him and your family.

God's way is to follow His Word. Get alone with Him, get into His Word, and let Him teach you His ways. You probably won't be a millionaire by next year. But you will be further ahead than you are right now if you do things His way. Besides, the goal is not to be a millionaire. The goal is to have a full supply—that's true prosperity. Far too few people have a full supply. God wants to change that. Let Him do it in you!

Chapter 3 Summary

Those who prosper are those who sow seed where God tells them—even in times of famine. Don't limit yourself to your job for your income. Get liberated! Expand the borders of your expectations! Believe God's Word over the fearful philosophies of the world. His truth trumps everything. He knows how to prosper you and will reveal His plan to you as you seek Him and meditate on His Word. You are blessed to be a blessing. Sow the seed He has given you and stay in your gift. God will prosper you from the inside out as you focus on prospering your soul.

CHAPTER 4

Jesus Was Not Poor

Was Jesus rich? Good question. Many people, including theologians, would say, "No, He wasn't rich because He was born in a stable. Others say, "No, He wasn't rich because He didn't have a place to lay His head" (see Matthew 8:20). But their arguments that Jesus was poor are based on assumptions and incorrect interpretations of a few scriptures they have taken out of context.

In all my years of walking with the Lord, I have discovered that the best way to interpret Scripture is with Scripture. Instead of reading *into* the Word, we must *take from* the Word what it is saying. When it comes to clarifying the true meaning, the context or surrounding verses must be considered.

Let's take a few minutes to look at some key passages and allow them to speak for themselves as to whether Jesus was poor or not.

Why Does the Scripture Say, "Jesus Became Poor for Our Sakes?"

There is a verse in 2 Corinthians that many have misinterpreted or misunderstood. Take a moment to carefully read it and receive its meaning at face value.

> **2 CORINTHIANS 8:9**
> **9 For ye know the grace of our Lord Jesus Christ, that, though he was rich, yet for your sakes he became poor, that ye through his poverty might be rich.**

This verse tells us that Jesus *was* rich. What it doesn't specifically tell us is *when* He was rich.

What else can we learn from this verse? Jesus at some point became poor, and there was a reason He became poor: It was for your sake and my sake.

Think about this in terms of a natural family. If my wife and I became poor for the sake of our children, how would that really help them? The only way it could help our children is if we became poor *after* giving all our riches to them. That's what Jesus did for us.

He didn't become poor because being poor made Him humble, spiritual, or closer to God. He also didn't become poor because being poor is holy. Jesus became poor so that you and I might become rich through His poverty.

Something else worth noting about 2 Corinthians 8:9 is the original meaning of two key words. Again, the Scripture says, "yet for your sakes he became poor, that ye through his poverty might be rich." The word *poverty* is the Greek word *ptocheia*, which means "beggary, indigence, poverty." Thayer's Greek-English Lexicon defines this word *ptocheia* as "the condition of one destitute of riches and abundance." That's what Jesus became for us, *ptocheia*—He became destitute of riches and abundance.

Why did He do it? The answer is found in the phrase *might be rich*. These three words together are the Greek word *plouteo*, which means "to become wealthy, to be increased with goods, to be made rich." Jesus became destitute of riches and abundance, basically poverty-stricken, so that we might become wealthy and increased with goods.

What Does the Scripture Mean, "Jesus Became Sin for Us?"

Now let's look at another verse that has a similar principle in it.

> **2 CORINTHIANS 5:21**
> **21 For he hath made him to be sin for us, who knew no sin; that we might be made the righteousness of God in him.**

God the Father made His sinless Son, Jesus, to be sin for us. He didn't make Jesus sin because being sinful is holy or humble. He made Jesus to be sin for us so that we could become righteous. Jesus became our substitute. He bore our sins and the sins of the world upon Himself and gave us His righteousness! I like to call this "the big switcheroo!"

Can you see the connection between 2 Corinthians 8:9 and 5:21? Jesus who was rich became poor so that we might become rich. Likewise, He was righteous and without sin but became sin so that we might become righteous. Jesus became our substitute; He submitted to the Father's will and bore the curse of sin and poverty upon Himself to give us His riches! The poor become rich and the unrighteous become righteous through Him.

How Is Healing a Part of Prosperity?

Jesus did not only become poor so that we might be rich, and become sin that we might be righteous. He also took on all our sickness that we might receive His healing. This too is a part of His substitutionary work.

> **ISAIAH 53:4-5**
> **4 Surely he hath borne our griefs, and carried our sorrows: yet we did esteem him stricken, smitten of God, and afflicted.**
> **5 But he was wounded for our transgressions, he was bruised for our iniquities: the chastisement of our peace was upon him; and with his stripes we are healed.**

God, speaking through Isaiah, is *not* just referring to spiritual healing in these verses. He is specifically referring to *physical healing*. Matthew clearly gives evidence to this fact in his gospel account saying,

> **MATTHEW 8:16-17** *(NKJV)*
> **16 When evening had come, they brought to Him many who were demon-possessed. And He cast out**

the spirits with a word, and healed all who were sick,
17 That it might be fulfilled which was spoken by Isaiah the prophet, saying: "He Himself took our infirmities and bore our sicknesses."

Jesus took our sickness and gave us His healing. To make sure we get this powerful principle, Peter also quotes from Isaiah 53 declaring, "...by whose stripes ye were *healed*" (1 Peter 2:24). The word *healed* here is the Greek word *iaomai*—a word derived from the medical term used to describe "the physical healing or curing of the human body." Make no mistake, physical healing is an inseparable part of God's prosperity. It is yours by faith. Claim it in the name of Jesus!

According to the Old Testament, Why Was Jesus Blessed?

Many believe that Jesus was poor during His earthly ministry, but that cannot be true. Why? Because Jesus lived a perfect life. He honored and obeyed all the commandments of God the Father, and as a result He reaped the reward of obedience outlined in the law.

Hebrews 4:15 says that Jesus "...was in all points tempted like as we are, *yet without sin*." He is the only person in history to ever live a perfect life. He was completely without sin, and completely obedient to the Heavenly Father. According to Deuteronomy 28, the person who follows and completely obeys the commands of the Lord will be blessed. Verses 1-14 list the blessings, and they include financial provision.

No one was ever able to completely keep the law, not even the God-honoring patriarchs like Abraham, Isaac, and Jacob. But even these patriarchs, who did their best to follow the law, were very blessed while here on earth.

Therefore, if the patriarchs, who kept most of the law, were blessed, then Jesus who kept *all* of the law completely must have been exceedingly blessed. If He was *not* rich, then God lied in Deuteronomy 28. But God did *not* lie. As the Scripture says,

> **NUMBERS 23:19** *(NKJV)*
> **19 God is not a man, that He should lie, nor a son of man, that He should repent. Has He said, and will He not do? Or has He spoken, and will He not make it good?**

If God said those who obey Him will live an abundantly blessed, rich life, they will.

What Does It Mean to Be Rich?

So what exactly does it mean to be rich? Being rich or blessed does not necessarily mean having a lot of money stored in a bank somewhere. Rich simply means "to have a *full* supply." Again, we serve a God of *more-than-enough*, not a God of barely-get-by. More-than-enough means having a full supply of what you need when you need it. This is the kind of life Jesus lived.

When it was time for Jesus to pay His taxes, we can assume from Scripture that He didn't have any cash on hand. However, He knew He had access to the Father's full supply. And because He listened to and fully trusted

His Father, He received direction for Peter to go fishing for the finances. Miraculously, the first fish Peter caught had enough money in its mouth to pay both of their taxes. Now that's an example of full supply! (See the whole story in Matthew 17:24-27.)

Being rich simply means having a full supply of what you need when you need it.

On two separate occasions, Jesus fed multitudes of people with only a few fish and a few loaves of bread. He didn't have a large supply of food in storage, but He knew He had access to His Father's inheritance of provision. When He took what He had, gave thanks to the Father, and blessed it, the power of God supernaturally multiplied His supply. A few loaves and a few fish turned into *more than enough* food. It fed about 15,000 people on one occasion and about 12,000 people on another (see Matthew 14:15-21; 15:32-38).

This is what it means to be rich in God's economy. It is having a full supply of what you need when you need it. This is the kind of life Jesus lived, and it's the kind of life you are meant to live in Him.

Did You Know That Jesus Had a Treasurer?

Most sound organizations have at least three officers that oversee its business: a president, a vice president, and a treasurer. The treasurer is the one I want to zero in on because he is responsible for the money. Jesus had such a person on His team. Who was Jesus' treasurer? The beloved apostle John reveals him as he retells the story of the Last Supper:

> **JOHN 13:27-30** *(NKJV)*
> **27** Now after the piece of bread, Satan entered him {*Judas Iscariot*}. Then Jesus said to him, "What you do, do quickly."
> **28** But no one at the table knew for what reason He said this to him.
> **29** For some thought, because Judas had the money box, that Jesus had said to him, "Buy those things we need for the feast," or that he should give something to the poor.
> **30** Having received the piece of bread, he then went out immediately. And it was night.

Judas was in charge of all the money for Jesus' ministry. In order for him to be in control of money, there had to be money for him to be in control of. If Jesus was poor, He certainly wouldn't need a treasurer. He also would not have been able to support twelve men and their families as they traveled with Him in the ministry.

But that's not all. In addition to the Twelve, Jesus probably had a number of others who assisted Him in ministry of whom we have no record. He took care of all their needs too. Without question, money was needed to make the ministry of Jesus possible.

Where Did Jesus Get the Money to Minister?

From Jewish custom, we understand that a Jewish man became a rabbi around the age of thirty. Once Jesus reached this age, His work as a carpenter ceased.

It had to in order for Him to fully devote Himself to the business of His heavenly Father. This means His ministry was not self-funded. Where do you suppose Jesus got all the money He needed? Luke sheds light on the source:

> **LUKE 8:1-3**
> 1 And it came to pass afterward, that he went throughout every city and village, preaching and showing the glad tidings of the kingdom of God: and the twelve were with him,
> 2 And certain women, which had been healed of evil spirits and infirmities, Mary called Magdalene, out of whom went seven devils,
> 3 And Joanna the wife of Chuza Herod's steward, and Susanna, and many others, which *ministered unto him of their substance.*

Did you catch that? He had many followers who contributed to His support. The Amplified translation puts it this way:

> **LUKE 8:3** *(AMP)*
> 3 And Joanna, the wife of Chuza, Herod's household manager; and Susanna; and many others, who ministered to and *provided for Him and them* out of their property and personal belongings.

We know that on one occasion, Mary, the sister of Lazarus, poured expensive ointment on Jesus. When she performed this act of love, Judas became indignant, arguing that the perfume should have been sold and the money from the sale given to the poor. The apostle John writes:

> **JOHN 12:3-8** *(NKJV)*
> 3 Then Mary took a pound of very costly oil of spikenard, anointed the feet of Jesus, and wiped His feet with her hair. And the house was filled with the fragrance of the oil.
> 4 But one of His disciples, Judas Iscariot, Simon's son, who would betray Him, said,
> 5 "Why was this fragrant oil not sold for three hundred denarii and given to the poor?"
> 6 This he said, not that he cared for the poor, but because he was a thief, and had the money box; and he used to take what was put in it.
> 7 But Jesus said, "Let her alone; she has kept this for the day of My burial.
> 8 For the poor you have with you always, but Me you do not have always."

Pure spikenard was imported from the mountains of India and very costly. Many Bible scholars believe that this pound of ointment was worth an entire year's wages. That is about how much money 300 denarii was equivalent to. That was expensive perfume! Obviously, Mary wasn't poor because poor people don't have perfume worth one year's wages.

Now here is where a rational mind has to take a back seat to the ways of the Spirit. Notice that Jesus did not rebuke Mary for her actions. Instead, He rebuked the disciple who complained about it.

Ironically, this type of scenario still plays out today. Whenever a preacher receives an expensive gift, someone will invariably pipe up and say, "They shouldn't have that! They don't need something that expensive. They should sell it and give the money to the poor!" In many cases, the same people who make these statements usually don't give anything to the poor.

Jesus believed in helping the poor, but He didn't believe in helping the poor while neglecting to bless the preacher. Yes, there have been some ministers of the gospel who have mishandled the blessings of God. Nevertheless, God wants His ministers provided for. When Jesus sent out the Twelve to heal the sick and cast out evil spirits, He said,

> **MATTHEW 10:9-10** *(NLT)*
> 9 "Don't take any money in your money belts—no gold, silver, or even copper coins.
> 10 Don't carry a traveler's bag with a change of clothes and sandals or even a walking stick. Don't hesitate to accept hospitality, because those who work deserve to be fed."

And through the apostle Paul, God declares,

> **1 TIMOTHY 5:17-18** *(AMP)*
> 17 Let the elders who perform the duties of their office well be considered doubly worthy of honor [and of adequate financial support], especially those who labor faithfully in preaching and teaching.
> 18 For the Scripture says, You shall not muzzle an ox when it is treading out the grain, and again, The laborer is worthy of his hire.

Make no mistake. Jesus and His workers were provided for abundantly, and a good portion of that provision came from among those He ministered to.

Jesus believed in helping the poor, but He didn't believe in helping the poor while neglecting to bless the preacher.

What About the Disciples? Were They Poor?

In case you wondered, the disciples weren't poor either! I'll prove it to you through these words penned in the Gospel of Mark:

> **MARK 10:24-27**
> **24 And the disciples were astonished at his words. But Jesus answereth again, and saith unto them, Children, how hard is it for them that trust in riches to enter into the kingdom of God!**
> **25 It is easier for a camel to go through the eye of a needle, than for a rich man to enter into the kingdom of God.**
> **26 And they were *astonished out of measure*, saying among themselves, Who then can be saved?**
> **27 And Jesus looking upon them saith, With men it is impossible, but not with God: for with God all things are possible.**

Notice that the disciples were "astonished out of measure" when they heard Jesus saying this. If they had been poor, their response would have probably been a hearty "Amen!" But it wasn't. Instead, they were deeply perplexed and wondered greatly how anyone on earth could be saved. I believe this was a challenging statement for them because none of them was poor.

Here's something else to consider: All but one of the disciples were Jewish, and Jewish people are known throughout history to be excellent when it comes to business and matters of money. My wife grew up and went to school in a large Jewish community. She said she has never met one Jew who was poor. As a matter of fact, they all had the finest clothes, the most expensive jewelry, and the best hairstyles! The Jews have never believed in poverty. They have always believed in the blessing of Deuteronomy 28!

So if Jesus didn't become poor when He came to earth, when did He become poor? He became poor *after He was arrested*. At that point, the soldiers took everything He had and gambled for His clothes (see John 19:23-24). He was stripped of all His worldly possessions and treated like a notorious criminal. He became our substitute, paying the penalty for your sin, my sin, and the sin of all mankind. He who knew no sin became sin on the cross so that we might become the righteousness of God.

Everything that Adam lost through disobedience in the Garden of Eden, Jesus regained through obedience in the Garden of Gethsemane as He yielded His will to the will of the Father. Now that is the GRACE of God— God's **R**iches **A**t Christ's **E**xpense. Praise the wonderful name of Jesus!

Chapter 4 Summary

Jesus became poor so that you and I might become rich through His poverty. God made Him who knew no sin to be sin so that we could become His righteousness. Physical healing is also an inseparable part of God's prosperity. It is ours by faith just as all His other blessings. Being rich or blessed simply means having a full supply of what you need when you need it. This is the kind of life Jesus lived. He believed in helping the poor, but He didn't believe in helping the poor while neglecting to bless God's ministers. Everything Adam lost through disobedience in the Garden of Eden, Jesus regained through obedience in the Garden of Gethsemane. Praise His mighty Name!

CHAPTER 5

Abraham's Blessings Are Yours

There are fifteen different covenants in the Old Testament. And one of those covenants was made between God and Abraham. You can find the detailed account in Genesis 15. The Abrahamic covenant was created before the Law was given to Moses and the nation of Israel. The Law is what we often refer to as the *Old Covenant*. The *New Covenant* is what we have through Jesus Christ.

So what is a covenant? It is a special agreement made between two parties in which each person pledges to defend, protect, and provide for the other. The enemies of one party become the enemies of the other. Likewise, they also share each other's resources. To seal a covenant, one or more animals are sacrificed and prepared as a meal for the parties to share. Although many in the Western world are not familiar with this type of agreement, covenants are a regular occurrence in the East.

While the New Covenant through Christ nullified the sacrificial system of the Old Covenant through Moses, it did *not* nullify the Abrahamic covenant. God is still honoring His agreement. Why? Because Jesus Christ is a fulfillment of that agreement. The Word of God declares,

> **GALATIANS 3:29**
> **29 And if ye be Christ's, then are ye Abraham's seed, and heirs according to the promise.**

Through faith in Jesus Christ, you and I are partakers of the Abrahamic covenant. Therefore, Abraham's blessings are *your* blessings!

God Called and Made a Covenant with Abram

Interestingly, Jews, Muslims, and Christians all claim Abraham as their father, and rightly so. Abraham was the grandfather of Jacob, whom God changed his name to Israel (see Genesis 32:28). He is also the father of Ishmael, the patriarch of the twelve Arab princes whose descendants eventually founded the Muslim religion. And Abraham is a great forefather in the lineage of Jesus Christ; forty-two generations separate him from Christ (see Matthew 1).

God first appeared to Abram (his name before God changed it) when he was living in the land of Ur (see Acts 7:2-4). He appeared to him again in Haran and reiterated His call. The Scripture says,

> **GENESIS 12:1-3**
> **1 Now the Lord had said unto Abram, Get thee out of thy country, and from thy kindred, and from thy father's house, unto a land that I will show thee:**

> 2 And I will make of thee a great nation, and I will bless thee, and make thy name great; and thou shalt be a blessing:
> 3 And I will bless them that bless thee, and curse him that curseth thee: and in thee shall all families of the earth be blessed.

What did Abram do? He obeyed God. He left Haran and headed toward the land of Canaan. He was seventy-five years old when God called him. Shortly after he left Haran, God made a covenant with him, expanding the details of His blessing to include "offspring more numerous than the stars" (Genesis 15:5). What was Abram's response?

> **GENESIS 15:6**
> 6 And he believed in the Lord; and he counted it to him for righteousness.

Abram was counted as righteous because of his faith. He believed and trusted the Lord, and was called the father of faith. As we believe and trust in the promises of God, we position ourselves to inherit the blessings of Abraham.

He Was a God-Made Man

According to these verses, God promised to bless Abram greatly. Notice that Abram did not vow to make himself great; it was God doing the talking. Abram was *not* a self-made man, but a God-made man.

God told Abram, "I will make of thee a great nation, and I will bless thee, and make thy name great" (Genesis

12:2). Obviously, God has lived up to His promises. He has indeed made Abraham's descendants a great nation and made his name great. Think about it. It's been about 4,000 years since God spoke this, and we are still talking about Abraham today!

Now, some have thought, *Well, the blessing God spoke of wasn't financial. It was spiritual.* Yes, the blessings Abraham received included spiritual blessings, but as we read on, we see that they were also financial and material in nature. The Bible says,

> **GENESIS 13:2**
> **2 And Abram was very rich in cattle, in silver, and in gold.**

You can't get much clearer than that. Even in today's society, if you have a lot of livestock, silver, and gold, you would be rich too! Although it doesn't say exactly how much Abram had, we know it was a lot based on verses 5 and 6:

> **GENESIS 13:5-6**
> **5 And Lot also, which went with Abram, had flocks, and herds, and tents.**
> **6 And the land was not able to bear them, that they might dwell together: for *their substance was great*, so that they could not dwell together.**

Think about it. Through most of history, a person who had one or two key animals could take care of his family. But like Job, Abram had thousands of animals. Where did he get them? The same place he got all his possessions—God. God said He was going to bless Abram, and He did—big-time!

The blessings in Abram's life were so plentiful that they poured into Lot's life, too. Lot worked for Abram, and God blessed Lot for Abram's sake. It was a super cycle of abundance—more blessing than either of them could contain.

People put a premium on being self-made. God puts a premium on being God-made.

Not only did Abram's faith touch God's heart, but his *character* touched God's heart as well. Over the course of time, strife broke out between Lot and Abram's herdsmen. With godly wisdom and humility, Abram said to Lot,

> **GENESIS 13:8-9**
> **8 Let there be no strife, I pray thee, between me and thee, and between my herdmen and thy herdmen; for we be brethren.**
> **9 Is not the whole land before thee? Separate thyself, I pray thee, from me: if thou wilt take the left hand, then I will go to the right; or if thou depart to the right hand, then I will go to the left.**

Abram refused to live in strife and humbly preferred his nephew, Lot, over himself. God was deeply moved by Abram's character and blessed him accordingly. While Lot chose for himself the land he thought was best, Abram left the choosing up to God, and God promised to give him and his descendants "all the land he could see…forever" (see Genesis 13:15).

There was no selfish ambition in Abram's heart to climb the financial ladder, step on people, and gather stuff for himself. Instead, he trusted that his life was in God's hands and was abundantly blessed. People tend to put such a premium on being self-made. God puts a premium on being God-made!

I know that I'm not a self-made man. Everything good I have is from God. It's all because of His goodness and grace that I am blessed the way I am, and the same is true for you. Make no mistake:

JAMES 1:17 *(NKJV)*
17 Every good gift and every perfect gift is from above, and comes down from the Father of lights, with whom there is no variation or shadow of turning.

He Was Blessed to *Be* a Blessing

I said it before, but it bears repeating. God not only had plans to bless Abram, He also had plans to bless others through Abram. He said:

GENESIS 12:2-3
2 ...And thou shalt *be a blessing*:
3 And I will bless them that bless thee, and curse him that curseth thee: and in thee shall all families of the earth be blessed.

God said, "Not only am I going to bless you, Abram, but if anyone else blesses you, I am going to turn around and bless them as well! In fact, all the nations of the world will be blessed through you!" And that's exactly what God did.

The first person in Abraham's lineage to receive God's blessing and be a blessing was his son Isaac, the child of promise. For many years, Abraham poured wisdom and knowledge into him and helped connect him in relationship with God. Eventually he was on his own, cultivating a firsthand friendship with the God of his father. What were the results? The Bible says,

> **GENESIS 26:12-14**
> **12** Then Isaac sowed in that land, and received in the same year an hundredfold: and the Lord blessed him.
> **13** And the man waxed great, and went forward, and grew until he became very great:
> **14** For he had possession of flocks, and possessions of herds, and great store of servants: and the Philistines envied him.

Notice verse 12 says, "The *Lord* blessed him!" Like Abraham, Isaac was not a self-made man, but a God-made man. He was greatly blessed and highly favored of God.

Looking further down Abraham's family line we find Isaac's son, Jacob. As Abraham passed the blessing on to Isaac, so Isaac passed the blessing on to Jacob. He declared,

> **GENESIS 27:28-29**
> **28** Therefore God give thee of the dew of heaven, and the fatness of the earth, and plenty of corn and wine:

> **29** Let people serve thee, and nations bow down to thee: be lord over thy brethren, and let thy mother's sons bow down to thee: cursed be every one that curseth thee, and blessed be he that blesseth thee.
>
> **GENESIS 28:3-4**
> **3** And God Almighty bless thee, and make thee fruitful, and multiply thee, that thou mayest be a multitude of people;
> **4** And give thee the blessing of Abraham, to thee, and to thy seed with thee; that thou mayest inherit the land wherein thou art a stranger, which God gave unto Abraham.

Although Jacob tricked his father into giving him the rightful blessing of Esau, his older brother, God had ordained it to be that way from before their birth (see Genesis 25:23). According to God's plan, Jacob passed the blessing on to his sons.

Ultimately, all the nations of the world were blessed through Abraham. Without Abram doing what he did in obedience to God and each successive generation obediently doing their part, the door of blessing through their family would not have been opened for the Messiah to come to the earth. Thank God for obedient servants!

God Blesses Others for Our Sake

The blessings we receive are often for the sake of someone else. This principle is repeated throughout Scripture and clearly seen through the lives of the patriarchs. God said to Isaac, Abraham's son,

> **GENESIS 26:24**
> 24 ...I am the God of Abraham thy father: fear not, for I am with thee, and will bless thee, and multiply thy seed *for my servant Abraham's sake.*

So Isaac was blessed for Abraham's sake, and in the same way, so was Jacob. As a matter of fact, Lot and his family were not destroyed with the cities of Sodom and Gomorrah for the sake of Abraham. Genesis 19:29 says, "And it came to pass, when God destroyed the cities of the plain, that *God remembered Abraham*, and sent Lot out of the midst of the overthrow, when he overthrew the cities in which Lot dwelt." Wow! What a wonderful, covenant-keeping God we serve!

And His goodness doesn't stop. When we walk by faith and trust God daily as Abraham did, we too are blessed for Abraham's sake. At the same time, others are blessed for our sake. With the blessing of Abraham on our lives, even our employers will be blessed in all that we do. Laban, Jacob's father-in-law, is a perfect example.

Did you know that Laban was blessed abundantly for Jacob's sake? When Jacob had worked for Laban several years and was ready to move out on his own, Laban pleaded with him not to go. The Scripture says,

> **GENESIS 30:27**
> 27 And Laban said unto him, I pray thee, if I have found favour in thine eyes, tarry: for I have learned by experience that the Lord hath blessed me for thy sake.

Laban was blessed for Jacob's sake, and Jacob was blessed for Abraham's sake. The blessing of Abraham continued even in the lives of his great-grandchildren, including Joseph.

Joseph had several dreams from God, which he shared with his brothers who envied him. As a result, they sold him into slavery to get rid of him. At that point, it sure didn't look like Joseph had the blessing of Abraham on his life. But something supernatural happened in spite of all the evil done to him. The Bible says,

> **GENESIS 39:1-5**
> 1 And Joseph was brought down to Egypt; and Potiphar, an officer of Pharaoh, captain of the guard, an Egyptian, bought him of the hands of the Ishmeelites, which had brought him down thither.
> 2 And *the Lord was with Joseph*, and he was a prosperous man; and he was in the house of his master the Egyptian.
> 3 And his master saw that the Lord was with him, and that the Lord made all that he did to prosper in his hand.
> 4 And Joseph found grace in his sight, and he served him: and he made him overseer over his house, and all that he had he put into his hand.
> 5 And it came to pass from the time that he had made him overseer in his house, and over all that he had, that *the Lord blessed the Egyptian's house for Joseph's sake*; and the blessing of the Lord was upon all that he had in the house, and in the field.

Just as Laban was blessed for Jacob's sake, so Potiphar was blessed for Joseph's sake. Potiphar was an officer who was well aware of the characteristics that make a good servant. That's what he thought he was buying in Joseph, but he soon began to notice that Joseph was different. Success followed him everywhere he went! All Potiphar had to think about was what he wanted for dinner, because Joseph took care of everything else successfully.

Trust me, as you obediently walk in the footsteps of Abraham, and more importantly Jesus, blessings will chase you down; you won't have to chase them. Remember, the Scripture says, "...though he {Christ} was rich, yet for your sakes he became poor, that ye through his poverty might be rich" (2 Corinthians 8:9).

With Prosperity Often Comes Persecution

Okay, so how can you know you are starting to flow in the prosperity God has for you? A major clue is that people will start envying you. Jesus laid out this principle in the Gospel of Mark:

> **MARK 10:29-30**
> **29 And Jesus answered and said, Verily I say unto you, There is no man that hath left house, or brethren, or sisters, or father, or mother, or wife, or children, or lands, for my sake, and the gospel's,**
> **30 But he shall receive an hundredfold now in this time, houses, and brethren, and sisters, and mothers, and children, and lands, *with persecutions*....**

That is what happened to Jacob. The Scripture says,

GENESIS 30:43-31:2
43 And the man {*Jacob*} increased exceedingly, and had much cattle, and maidservants, and menservants, and camels, and asses.
1 And he heard the words of Laban's sons, saying, Jacob hath taken away all that was our father's; and of that which was our father's hath he gotten all this glory.
2 And Jacob beheld the countenance of Laban, and, behold, it was not toward him as before.

When Jacob began to prosper, Laban's sons grumbled and complained against him and Laban's attitude toward him turned unfavorable.

Similarly, when Joseph prospered in the favor of his father, his brothers hated him greatly. Jacob had twelve sons, and Joseph was the eleventh born. But He was the first born of Rachel, the wife he favored most. God's Word says,

GENESIS 37:3-4
3 Now Israel loved Joseph more than all his children, because he was the son of his old age: and he made him a coat of many colours.
4 And when his brethren saw that their father loved him more than all his brethren, they hated him, and could not speak peaceably unto him.

As previously stated, Joseph was sold into slavery. Then he eventually ended up in prison for a crime he didn't commit. Through it all, God blessed him more and more.

In prison, Joseph was highly favored by the jail keeper and promoted to overseer. And because of his ability to interpret dreams, he was remembered by Pharaoh's cupbearer when Pharaoh had a dream he didn't understand. When it seemed like Joseph was doomed to the dungeon for life, he was suddenly brought out to interpret Pharaoh's dream. What was the outcome? The Bible says,

> **GENESIS 41:38-43**
> 38 And Pharaoh said unto his servants, Can we find such a one as this is, a man in whom the Spirit of God is?
> 39 And Pharaoh said unto Joseph, Forasmuch as God hath shewed thee all this, there is none so discreet and wise as thou art:
> 40 Thou shalt be over my house, and according unto thy word shall all my people be ruled: only in the throne will I be greater than thou.
> 41 And Pharaoh said unto Joseph, See, I have set thee over all the land of Egypt.
> 42 And Pharaoh took off his ring from his hand, and put it upon Joseph's hand, and arrayed him in vestures of fine linen, and put a gold chain about his neck;
> 43 And he made him to ride in the second chariot which he had; and they cried before him, Bow the knee: and he made him ruler over all the land of Egypt.

From the prison to the palace—that's what can happen when the blessing of God is on a person's life! When God prospers us, we too will experience persecution. But if we endure, we will be blessed even more!

So don't be surprised when people turn ugly and begin to envy you when you prosper. Yes, they may say things like, "I don't think you should have that much! You're a Christian, aren't you? Well, I don't think a Christian should live in a house that nice or drive a car like that. You should take that money and give it to the poor." But don't let them get to you.

At the same time, be careful not to fall into the trap of envying those God is prospering. It is not our business to judge. On the contrary, we are to rejoice with them. God instructs us,

1 CORINTHIANS 12:26 *(NKJV)*
26 …If one member is honored, all the members rejoice with it.

I am filled with joy when people in my church are blessed! I am happy when my members get good jobs, promotions, and bonuses. I like to hear those testimonies just as much as I like giving them. So don't be jealous—be joyful when others prosper and succeed. Say, "I'm in that line to be blessed!" God is not a respecter of persons, and there are no shortages in heaven. Believe for the best; don't expect the worst.

Think Abundance, Not Shortage

Remember what Jesus said in John 10:10? He said, "The thief cometh not, but for to steal, and to kill, and to destroy: I am come that they might have life, and that they might have it more *abundantly*." God wants us to think in terms of abundance, not shortage.

Many believers do not have their minds renewed with God's Word, and as a result, they magnetically pick up the world's thinking that "there's just not enough money to go around." Naturally, when they see someone else prospering, they automatically think there is less for them. But that is simply not the case.

Regardless of what the economy is like, there is plenty of money to be made *right now*—this very day, this very year! What worked ten years ago may not work now, but there is something that will work and produce increase. God knows what it is, and He will reveal it to you as you live a life sensitive to the leading of His Holy Spirit. This is the key to gaining the needed knowledge and wisdom in every circumstance you face.

Realize that God doesn't make failures. He has *not* predetermined that one person will struggle his entire life while another lives prosperously. I don't see that in the Scriptures. Each person must choose to seek God in order to reap the blessings He has for his life. God will not force His blessings on you.

Let me be clear: No person can work and *earn* the blessings of God. However, God will bless the work of our hands! The Bible clearly teaches that we are supposed to work:

> **2 THESSALONIANS 3:10**
> 10 For even when we were with you, this we commanded you, that *if any would not work, neither should he eat.*

1 THESSALONIANS 4:11
11 And that ye study to be quiet, and to *do your own business*, and to *work with your own hands*, as we commanded you.

What is the scriptural purpose for working? God says through the apostle Paul,

EPHESIANS 4:28
28 Let him that stole steal no more: but rather let him labour, working with his hands the thing which is good, *that he may have to give to him that needeth.*

We work so that we have seed to help those in need around us. There is great reward in honest labor. At the same time, we must also leave room in our thinking for God to bless us apart from our job. God's resources are unlimited, and He can work in ways we could never dream of.

Pastors and business owners are looking for modern day Josephs. Are you a Joseph?

Be Faithful and God Will Promote You

As a New Testament, born-again believer, do people see anything different about you? They should! Joseph was not born again. He was operating under a weaker covenant than what we as believers have today, yet he was extremely prosperous and powerful in God's kingdom.

There are business owners and pastors everywhere who are looking for modern-day Josephs! These are people who can handle more responsibility and run things efficiently, even in the boss's absence. They act wisely and get promoted into higher positions of authority because of their faithfulness.

Joseph was promoted to the second-highest position in Egypt and given the Pharaoh's signet ring to secure whatever he needed. He was arrayed in the finest clothes money could buy. He wore a solid-gold chain around his neck and rode in the finest chariot in Egypt. I read recently that Bentley made two custom vehicles worth about $14 million for the Queen of England and her companions to ride in. In today's terms, that would be like Joseph getting to ride around in a $7 million car while he traveled with Pharaoh! I'll bet it was pretty nice!

Yes, Egypt was an ungodly nation. It represents the world system in which we live today—the world system of which Satan is the god (see 2 Corinthians 4:4). Isn't it amazing that God made Joseph second in command of this ungodly nation? He can do the same thing for you; He can promote you to a high position of authority even in our ungodly society. Why would He do such a thing? For the same reason He promoted Joseph: so that the lives of many people might be saved (see Genesis 50:20).

You may be thinking, *How can I be promoted at a minimum-wage job?* The answer is to become a Joseph. You will not continue making minimum wage if you develop his work ethic. As you are faithful with little, God will expand your influence and make you ruler over much (see Matthew 2:20-24). Eventually, you will be managing the place. And if you still cannot make a lot of money, God will move you to a better job. God always has a way!

So don't ever adopt the attitude that you are not going to work hard because you only get paid a small amount. It doesn't matter if you're working for free, for minimum wage, or for millions. You should always work like Joseph. I believe his work ethic is summed up in this passage:

> **COLOSSIANS 3:23-24** *(NKJV)*
> **23 And whatever you do, do it heartily, as to the Lord and not to men,**
> **24 Knowing that from the Lord you will receive the reward of the inheritance; for you serve the Lord Christ.**

Whatever you do, work hard at it because you're actually working for the Lord. Ask Him for the strength to have the best attitude you can. This will attract His blessings and promotions.

Don't spend your life complaining about injustices against you or making excuses for sloppy work. Serve your employer as if you are serving God. Make the best of every situation and you will rise to the top!

Remind God of His Covenant Promises

Is there lack in your life? Don't blame the economy. Turn off the news and get into God's Word! Again and again, our heavenly Father promises us that we are secure in Him as we reverentially fear Him and trust Him to provide. He says,

> **PSALM 34:9-10** *(NLT)*
> **9 Fear the Lord, you his godly people, for those who fear him will have all they need.**
> **10 Even strong young lions sometimes go hungry, but those who trust in the Lord will lack no good thing.**
>
> **PSALM 84:11** *(NKJV)*
> **11 ...No good thing will He withhold from those who walk uprightly.**

If you are a born-again believer in Christ, you are in God's family. He is your heavenly Father and is bound by His covenant to take care of you. You are in line to inherit the blessings of Abraham and Christ Himself.

> **GALATIANS 3:29**
> **29 And if ye be Christ's, then are ye Abraham's seed, and heirs according to the promise.**

Jesus came to give us the blessing of Abraham! Let this truth sink deep down into your soul and spirit:

> **GALATIANS 3:13-14**
> **13 Christ hath redeemed us from the curse of the law, being made a curse for us: for it is written, Cursed is every one that hangeth on a tree:**
> ***14 That the blessing of Abraham might come on the Gentiles through Jesus Christ;* that we might receive the promise of the Spirit through faith.**

Through faith in Christ, we are set free from the curse of poverty and made heirs of the blessing of Abraham, just like Isaac and Jacob.

Chapter 5 Summary

You are a partaker of the Abrahamic covenant; Abraham's blessings are your blessings! As you believe and trust in the promises of God, you position yourself to inherit those blessings. Not one of us is self-made; we are God-made. Every good and perfect gift is from Him! Just as Abraham was blessed to be a blessing, so are we. We are often blessed for the sake of others, and others are blessed for our sake. When God prospers us, we will experience persecution. But if we endure, we'll be blessed even more! Whatever you do, work hard at it because you're actually working for the Lord. Be faithful with what you have and where you are, and God will promote you!

CHAPTER 6

Get Wisdom and Understanding!

Prosperity clearly includes money. But prosperity is so much more than money and material possessions. Prosperity comes in many forms and provides countless blessings. One very valuable form of prosperity is *wisdom* and *understanding*. Knowledge is wonderful, but knowledge alone is incomplete. We need wisdom and understanding with it. Understanding enables us to comprehend knowledge, and wisdom is the ability to apply knowledge correctly.

The book of Proverbs is full of scriptures encouraging us to get wisdom and understanding like these found in chapter 4:

> **PROVERBS 4:5-8**
> 5 Get wisdom, get understanding: forget it not; neither decline from the words of my mouth.
> 6 Forsake her not, and she shall preserve thee: love her, and she shall keep thee.
> 7 Wisdom is the principal thing; therefore get wisdom: and with all thy getting get understanding.

> 8 Exalt her, and she shall promote thee: she shall bring thee to honour, when thou dost embrace her.

Wisdom and understanding are indeed true riches. Knowing what to do, and when and how to do it, is priceless. How valuable are wisdom and understanding to you? God's Word declares,

> **PROVERBS 3:13-15** *(NKJV)*
> 13 Happy is the man who finds wisdom, and the man who gains understanding;
> 14 For her proceeds are better than the profits of silver, and her gain than fine gold.
> 15 She is more precious than rubies, and all the things you may desire cannot compare with her.

Throughout the book of Proverbs, we are urged to get wisdom and understanding. When we pursue and receive these gifts from God, we have a prosperity that is unequalled.

Wisdom and understanding are true riches.

King Solomon: An Example of the Riches of Wisdom

Interestingly, God spoke and wrote the majority of the book of Proverbs through King Solomon, the wisest man to ever live aside from Jesus. His life gives us a great example of seeking and receiving godly wisdom and understanding.

Solomon was the son of King David, selected by God to take the throne of Israel just before David died. We know from Scripture that God blessed Solomon exceedingly, but the reason he was blessed with such prosperity is definitely worth noting. In 1 Kings 3:5 it is recorded that the Lord appeared to Solomon in a dream at night and asked him, "What do you want Me to give you?" Solomon's response is the reason the Lord blessed him so abundantly:

> **1 KINGS 3:9-13**
> 9 Give therefore thy servant an understanding heart to judge thy people, that I may discern between good and bad: for who is able to judge this thy so great a people?
> 10 And *the speech pleased the Lord*, that Solomon had asked this thing.
> 11 And God said unto him, Because thou hast asked this thing, and hast not asked for thyself long life; neither hast asked riches for thyself, nor hast asked the life of thine enemies; but hast asked for thyself understanding to discern judgment;
> 12 Behold, I have done according to thy words: lo, I have given thee a wise and an understanding heart; so that there was none like thee before thee, neither after thee shall any arise like unto thee.
> 13 And I have also given thee that which thou hast not asked, both riches, and honour: so that there shall not be any among the kings like unto thee all thy days.

Solomon didn't have a lust or greed for money, material gain, or fame. He didn't ask for long life, riches, or to get even with his enemies. He had a humble attitude, a right heart. He was thinking, *I'm just a kid. How can I possibly rule these people? I need wisdom!* His request really pleased the Lord. As a result, God not only gave him a wise and understanding heart, but also what he didn't ask for—riches and honor.

Whose idea was it to give Solomon riches? It was God's idea! The Bible says,

> **PSALM 35:27**
> **27 Let them shout for joy, and be glad, that favour my righteous cause: yea, let them say continually, Let the Lord be magnified, which hath pleasure in the prosperity of his servant.**

Prosperity is God's idea. He gives wisdom and understanding, along with riches, fame, and honor to those who love and honor Him with a humble heart. He takes pleasure in prospering His servants. Indeed, "...no good thing will he withhold from them that walk uprightly" (Psalm 84:11).

How Prosperous Was Solomon?

Out of all the kings of Israel, Solomon was the wealthiest. The Bible gives us some details about the resources with which God blessed him. Take a look at this impressive spread sheet out of the pages of 1 Kings and 1 Chronicles:

Annually, Solomon received about 25 tons of gold. (1 Kings 10:14)

His huge throne was decorated with ivory and overlaid with fine gold. (1 Kings 10:18)

All of his drinking cups and utensils were made of solid gold. (1 Kings 10:21)

He had 1,400 chariots and 12,000 horses. (1 Chronicles 1:14)

Silver was as plentiful and common in Jerusalem as rocks. (1 Kings 10:27)

Solomon had so much gold that he made 200 large shields out of it, each weighing over 15 pounds, and 300 small shields, each weighing about four pounds (see 1 Kings 10:16-17). These shields were not for battle, because gold is one of the softest metals on earth. Instead, they were made for decoration. The Scripture says,

> **2 CHRONICLES 9:22-23** *(NKJV)*
> **22 King Solomon surpassed all the kings of the earth in riches and wisdom.**
> **23 And all the kings of the earth sought the presence of Solomon to hear his wisdom, which God had put in his heart.**

Indeed, King Solomon was exceedingly blessed!

Godly Wisdom Attracts Others

When a person has true, godly wisdom and understanding, others are attracted to him. Solomon was no exception. Probably the most notable encounter he had was with the Queen of Sheba. Sheba is understood to be modern-day Ethiopia. The distance the queen traveled to meet Solomon is approximately 1,550 miles and would have taken quite a bit of time to accomplish. But she was willing to make the trip to see for herself if what she had heard of him was true. Scripture says,

> **1 KINGS 10:1-8**
> 1 And when the queen of Sheba heard of the fame of Solomon concerning the name of the Lord, she came to prove him with hard questions.
> 2 And she came to Jerusalem with a very great train, with camels that bare spices, and very much gold, and precious stones: and when she was come to Solomon, she communed with him of all that was in her heart.
> 3 And Solomon told her all her questions: there was not any thing hid from the king, which he told her not.
> 4 And when the queen of Sheba had seen all Solomon's wisdom, and the house that he had built,
> 5 And the meat of his table, and the sitting of his servants, and the attendance of his ministers, and their apparel, and his cupbearers, and his ascent by which he went up unto the house of the Lord; there was no more spirit in her.
> 6 And she said to the king, It was a true report that I heard in mine own land of thy acts and of thy wisdom.
> 7 Howbeit I believed not the words, until I came, and mine eyes had seen it: and, behold, the half was not told me: thy wisdom and prosperity exceedeth the fame which I heard.
> 8 Happy are thy men, happy are these thy servants, which stand continually before thee, and that hear thy wisdom.

When the Queen of Sheba saw the excellence and wealth of Solomon's kingdom and heard the wisdom he spoke, she was overwhelmed. She took special notice of the food on his table and the organization of his officials and servants. She was amazed by their splendid clothing and with their living quarters.

If you have ever seen a large, stately home that was built during the 1800s, you would probably have noticed the beautiful architectural design and spaciousness of the main house. But when you saw the servants' quarters, you would have noticed a stark contrast. They are usually plain, small, and unimpressive. Well, when the queen saw the servants' quarters in Solomon's house, she was impressed. For her to be impressed, they must have been of high caliber!

The queen also talked with Solomon about everything on her mind, and he had answers to all her questions; nothing was too hard for him to explain. "Thy wisdom and prosperity exceeds the fame which I heard," she exclaimed. "Happy are thy men, happy are these thy servants, which stand continually before thee, and that hear thy wisdom" (1 Kings 10:7-8). Oh, how true. As the Word of God says,

> **PROVERBS 10:11, 23** *(AMP)*
> 11 The mouth of the [uncompromisingly] righteous man is a well of life...
> 23 ...and godly Wisdom is pleasure and relaxation to a man of understanding.

Godly Wisdom Attracts Blessings

What did the Queen of Sheba do when she heard the wisdom of Solomon and saw how prosperous the Lord had made him? Like countless other dignitaries, she presented him with gifts:

> **1 KINGS 10:10**
> **10 And she gave the king an hundred and twenty talents of gold, and of spices very great store, and precious stones: there came no more such abundance of spices as these which the queen of Sheba gave to king Solomon.**

The queen obviously didn't give Solomon gifts because he needed them. She gave him gifts to *honor* him. This is the same reason we should be giving gifts today—to honor those who have been placed in our lives to impart wisdom, and have been a blessing to us. Although this practice is lacking in our culture, it is still customary in the East to bring a gift when you go before a great person. I believe that is the principle God gives us through the apostle Paul:

> **1 TIMOTHY 5:17** *(AMP)*
> **17 Let the elders who perform the duties of their office well be considered doubly *worthy of honor* [and of adequate financial support], especially those who labor faithfully in preaching and teaching.**

Clearly, when a man is gifted with godly wisdom, not only do people seek him out, they also seek to bless him. Think about it…

Joseph's gift of supernatural wisdom and insight into interpreting dreams opened the door for him to be made second in command of Egypt—the most powerful nation on the face of the earth at that time. God moved on Pharaoh's heart, and he blessed Joseph exceedingly (see Genesis 41:41-44).

Daniel's gifts of great wisdom, insight, and administration opened the door for him to serve in the highest areas of leadership under the kings of Babylon and Persia for nearly 80 years. When Daniel interpreted King Nebuchadnezzar's dream, God moved on the king's heart, and he blessed Daniel exceedingly (see Daniel 2:46-49).

When a man is gifted with godly wisdom, not only do people seek him out, they also seek to bless him.

The Word of God declares:

PROVERBS 18:16
16 A man's gift maketh room for him, and bringeth him before great men.

As you seek and receive the riches of godly wisdom and understanding, others will be attracted to you and desire to bless you. It will take time. It did for Joseph, Daniel, and Solomon. But God will honor His Word. In the meantime, remember to bless and honor those around you who have imparted things from God to you, and have been a blessing in your life.

One Greater Than Solomon Lives in You

No doubt, Solomon was one of the greatest kings that ever lived. He was certainly the wisest. God told him, "I have given thee a wise and an understanding heart; so that there was none like thee before thee, neither after thee shall any arise like unto thee" (1 Kings 3:12).

Indeed, Solomon's wisdom and greatness has been known far and wide for many generations. Even Jesus had something interesting to say about him, something His listeners did not expect to hear:

> **MATTHEW 12:42**
> **42 The queen of the south shall rise up in the judgment with this generation, and shall condemn it: for she came from the uttermost parts of the earth to hear the wisdom of Solomon; and, behold, a greater than Solomon is here.**

Jesus acknowledged that Solomon was great, but then He declared that He was greater than Solomon. Of course Jesus was greater. He is God in the flesh. You can't get any greater than that!

What's really amazing is that Jesus, the Greater One, has chosen to live in us! That's right. If you are a born-again child of God, *He lives in you*! And because He lives in you, He makes you great too! The Bible says, "...you are in Christ Jesus, who became for us **wisdom** from God..." (1 Corinthians 1:30 NKJV). You are exceedingly blessed because the Great I Am, the Creator of heaven and earth, lives inside of you!

> **COLOSSIANS 1:27** *(The Message)*
> **27 God wanted everyone, not just Jews, to know this rich and glorious secret inside and out, regardless of their background, regardless of their religious standing. The mystery in a nutshell is just this:**

Christ is in you, so therefore you can look forward to sharing in God's glory.

You can't help but be blessed with the Greater One living in you! Jesus came to give you an abundant life. Believe it. Receive it. Live it!

Chapter 6 Summary

Prosperity comes in many forms, including wisdom and understanding. These are true riches we are to seek. King Solomon's life is a great example of the riches of wisdom and understanding. It was God's idea to prosper him. He takes pleasure in prospering His servants. As we seek and receive wisdom and understanding, others will be attracted to us and want to bless us. Jesus has been made wisdom to us and has chosen to live in us. We can't help but be blessed!

CHAPTER 7

Prosperity Has a Purpose

Is the reality that God truly loves you and wants you to prosper sinking in yet? God wants to bless you more than you want to be blessed, but you have to believe it in order to receive it. Jesus died and rose again that you might have an *abundant* life, and it is not just for you and your family. It's for all the people God places in your path and allows your life to touch.

Prosperity has a purpose that reaches beyond the four walls of your house and mine. Like Abraham, God wants to bless you to *be* a blessing to others. And one of the greatest ways to be a blessing is to use what God has blessed you with to advance His kingdom on earth. That is the greatest purpose of prosperity and the focus of this chapter.

God Gives You the Power to Get Wealth

A very important principle of prosperity is found in the book of Deuteronomy. It reveals both the *source* and the *purpose* of prosperity. The Scripture says,

DEUTERONOMY 8:18
18 But thou shalt remember the Lord thy God: for it is he that giveth thee power to get wealth, that he may establish his covenant which he sware unto thy fathers, as it is this day.

Who gives you the power to get wealth? Does Scripture say it's the devil? A thousand times NO! God is the one who gives you power to get wealth. Why? Is it for you to buy a bigger television, a bigger house, a newer car, or take more vacations? Is it to do everything you always wanted to do, and then give a tip to the church and $10 to the missionary? No! God says He gives you the power to get wealth for the purpose of establishing HIS covenant.

Don't miss this point. I believe it is a major key to demolishing wrong mindsets that hinder God's blessings. God wants you to be blessed and enjoy nice things. I spent time laying out the history of the Old Testament saints, like Abraham and Job, so that you could know that having abundance is part of God's will. But the primary purpose of prosperity is to *establish His covenant with the people of the earth.*

To help you understand this verse, let's look at a couple of key words in the original Hebrew. The word *wealth* can be translated as "resources, riches, power, and strength," and the word *establish* means to "confirm, perform, make good, and strengthen." So under the Old Covenant, God gave His people the power to get wealth (resources, riches, power, and strength) in order to establish (confirm, perform, and make good) His covenant with Abraham and his descendants.

God's Primary Purpose of Prosperity: Spread the Gospel

Now you may be thinking, *But that's the Old Testament. How does God's promise in Deuteronomy affect us living in New Testament times?* Good point; and the answer is that His purpose remains the same. God is the same yesterday, today, and forever (see Hebrews 13:8). He gave His people power to get wealth then, and He gives His people power to get wealth now and forever. Why? He wants to establish His *new* covenant with the people of the earth. This is the covenant we have with God through Jesus Christ, His Son. The resources, riches, power, and strength He provides are to be used to fulfill Jesus' Great Commission:

MARK 16:15
15 And he said unto them, Go ye into all the world, and preach the gospel to every creature.

Think about it. Why did Jesus come?

1 TIMOTHY 1:15
15 This is a faithful saying, and worthy of all acceptation, that Christ Jesus came into the world to save sinners....

Jesus came into the world to save sinners. You and I could not work our way into right relationship with God the Father, so God came to us in the form of man—the Man Christ Jesus. He lived a sinless life and willingly surrendered it as the perfect sacrifice to pay the penalty for all our sin—past, present, and future. God raised Christ from the dead and did not allow His perfect Son to experience corruption. He seated Him at His right hand, and Jesus is now ever interceding (praying) for our well-being.

Make no mistake. Jesus wants *everyone* to receive Him and believe in Him as their Lord and Savior. The Bible declares,

> **2 PETER 3:9**
> **9 The Lord is not slack concerning his promise, as some men count slackness; but is longsuffering to us-ward, not willing that any should perish, but that all should come to repentance.**

So what is prosperity for? Primarily to enable us to get the gospel out so that people will not perish! Yes, God wants His children to enjoy nice things, but that is not His primary purpose. Get the big picture! God gives you the power to get wealth first and foremost so that you will financially support the spreading of the gospel. To obey Jesus' Great Commission, it takes money. God is ready, willing, and able to get you what you need and provide extra to advance His kingdom!

God gives you the power to get wealth primarily to support the spreading of the gospel.

God's Secondary Purpose of Prosperity: Teach All Nations

Spreading the good news of Jesus Christ in order to see people saved is "part 1" of the Great Commission. The second part is *teaching* those same people to observe and obey all that Jesus taught. Listen to His parting words to His disciples:

> **MATTHEW 28:19-20**
> 19 Go ye therefore, and *teach all nations*, baptizing them in the name of the Father, and of the Son, and of the Holy Ghost:
> 20 Teaching them to observe all things whatsoever I have commanded you: and, lo, I am with you always, even unto the end of the world. Amen.

The Great Commission is not just to preach to sinners, but also **to teach believers to observe all things that Jesus has commanded us.** Preachers are to teach believers to learn and put into practice everything the Word of God says! In this way they become doers and not just hearers. They learn to hold fast, keep, and watch what they are taught. As a pastor, that is why I keep our church doors open and teach God's Word two to three times a week. It is also why we bring in people with other ministry gifts to equip believers.

Think about it. What is the purpose of teaching people godly knowledge if they are not going to put it into practice? Preachers don't teach believers the Bible so they can heap up knowledge and win game show contests or excel at knowing trivia. We are not in a contest, and we are not studying Scripture to earn degrees and put certificates and trophies on display. The whole purpose of learning is so that we can live like Christ by the power of His Spirit and be a blessing to others.

God really brings this point home through James, instructing us to…

JAMES 1:22-25 *(NKJV)*
22 Be doers of the word, and not hearers only, deceiving yourselves.
23 For if anyone is a hearer of the word and not a doer, he is like a man observing his natural face in a mirror;
24 For he observes himself, goes away, and immediately forgets what kind of man he was.
25 But he who looks into the perfect law of liberty and continues in it, and is not a forgetful hearer but a doer of the work, this one will be blessed in what he does.

Learning to be doers of the Word and not hearers only happens as God's ministers faithfully teach and preach His Word and the Holy Spirit gives us understanding. Next to spreading the gospel, this is God's purpose for prospering His people. How long will God's purpose for prosperity remain in effect? Scripture says,

MATTHEW 24:14
14 And this gospel of the kingdom shall be preached in all the world for a witness unto all nations; and then shall the end come.

How Should You Respond to God's Blessings?

If you are walking in obedience to the truth God has revealed to you, He is going to prosper you. It's only a matter of time. The question is, how should you respond when He does?

Imagine you get a raise or receive an unexpected monetary blessing of considerable size. What thoughts cross your mind? Do you rejoice because you can support another missionary, give more to your church, or bless your pastor? Or do you get excited because you can finally buy the latest and greatest high-tech toy you've been wanting? Extra provision will reveal your heart's condition. I'm not saying this to bring condemnation, but to reveal our need for the mind of Christ in this area.

Jesus said, "Don't worry about what you're going to eat, what you're going to drink, or what you're going to wear. God knows what you need and He will provide it when you need it." Instead, He wants us to put God's agenda *first*:

> **MATTHEW 6:33**
> **33 But seek ye first the kingdom of God, and His righteousness; and all these things shall be added unto you.**

I like the way the Amplified version translates this verse:

> **MATTHEW 6:33** *(AMP)*
> **33 But seek (aim at and strive after) first of all His kingdom and His righteousness (*His way of doing and being right*), and then all these things taken together will be given you besides.**

Our focus should not be on getting more things or more money. Our focus should be on establishing God's kingdom—His way of doing and being right in all areas of our lives. When we do that, **then** all the things we need will be given to us when we need them.

> **Our focus should not be on getting more things or more money. It should be on establishing God's kingdom.**

When God blesses you, He has a plan for that provision. Many times His plan is for you to use it to meet your needs. Actually, it would be an exception if He asked you to give all of it away. He knows you have needs, and He has promised to meet them. But you must always be open and prayerful about what the blessing is to be used for before spending it.

Whatever you have, you should always hold it loosely. Be willing and ready to sell or give it away for God's purposes if He prompts you. If God has put it in your heart to give something away or sell it, obey Him. It will no longer be a blessing to you if you keep it. Don't be afraid. God's ways are always better, and He has a reward waiting for you on the other side!

All believers are called to give, but there are some who actually have a *ministry* of giving. The apostle Paul talks about this in Romans 12:8. These people are not financially broke, only wishing they could give. On the contrary, they are people whom God has made rich. They know how to make money and they love to invest it in others. They continually sow and reap blessings upon blessings. We need more people like this in the body of Christ.

Praying and believing God for the things you need is scriptural. You *should* be believing Him to supply all your needs. At the same time, you should also be believing Him to supply someone else's needs. I have discovered that when I'm in a jam, if I will help someone else out of a jam, God will help me. I know this may be hard for some to grasp, but it's true. Ask God for His grace to understand this revelation. Once you do, giving to God's kingdom and those around you will become exciting and productive in your life. Remember, you are blessed to *be* a blessing!

Believe God to Prosper You... For His Kingdom Purposes

Always remember that God is the One who gives you the power to get wealth—not the enemy, you, or anyone else. His primary purpose for prosperity is to spread the gospel of Jesus Christ and teach believers the truth so that they can become mature sons and daughters of God. If you have been saved for many years and you have not increased at all, you either haven't known about this aspect of the gospel or you are not obeying God in this area.

I challenge you to believe God to prosper you, not for self-serving reasons but to serve God. As the writer of Hebrews says,

> **HEBREWS 13:5 *(AMP)***
> 5 Let your character or moral disposition *be free from love of money* [including greed, avarice, lust, and craving for earthly possessions] and be satisfied

with your present [circumstances and with what you have]....

As you put the advancement of God's kingdom first in your life, you put yourself in a position for Him to prosper you. Don't wait until you are wealthy to give. Begin to give now and watch how God provides for you!

Chapter 7 Summary

God wants to bless you more than you want to be blessed, but you must believe it to receive it. He is the One who gives you the power to get wealth, and His primary purpose for prosperity is to establish His covenant with the people of the earth. This purpose includes two parts: spreading the gospel and teaching and making disciples of all nations. Our focus should never be on getting more things or more money. It should be on establishing God's kingdom. If God has put it in your heart to give something away or sell it, obey Him. He has a reward waiting for you on the other side!

Chapter 8

Get Your Soul in Gear!

One of the foundational scriptures on prosperity is found in 3 John 2. We have mentioned it before, but it is worth mentioning again. The King James Version reads,

> **3 JOHN 2**
> **2 Beloved, I wish *above all things* that thou mayest prosper and be in health, even as thy soul prospereth.**

And the New King James says,

> **3 JOHN 2 *(NKJV)***
> **2 Beloved, I pray that you may prosper *in all things* and be in health, just as your soul prospers.**

From these two versions of Scripture, we can see that God wants us to prosper *above all things* and *in all things*, even as our soul prospers. What is our soul? It is our mind, will, and emotions. Although it is invisible to the eye, the soul is vital to the quality of our Christian walk.

Man is threefold: spirit, soul, and body. When we repent of our sins and invite Jesus into our lives, we are saved. Instantly, our *spirit* is born again and the fullness of Christ's Spirit comes to live in us. This is called *justification*—it is just as if you never sinned.

Our soul, on the other hand, is not instantly saved. It is a *process* that takes time. The saving work of Jesus Christ transforms our mind, will, and emotions (our soul) to think, choose, and feel like Jesus little by little. This process is called *sanctification* and is done by the Holy Spirit (the Spirit of Christ) as we walk daily in fellowship with Him and feed on His Word.

Our prosperity from God is going to be in proportion to the prosperity, or spiritual health and maturity, of our soul. If you are not prospering in your soul, God cannot prosper you anywhere else. With this understanding, the prosperity of our soul becomes our number one priority, as it should be. Godly riches follow godly order.

Our prosperity from God is going to be in proportion to the prosperity, or spiritual health and maturity, of our soul.

Stop and Take an Internal Inventory...

Ask yourself, "How prosperous is my soul? How prosperous are my mind, will, and emotions? How much do I think, act, and feel the way God does about things? Do I have control over my thoughts, decisions, and feelings, or are they controlling me?" God desires your born-again spirit to control your soul by the power of His Spirit. As we learned earlier, feeding yourself God's Word is a major key to experiencing this in your life.

Make no mistake about it! God wants you to prosper in all things and be in health, but He will only allow it to the degree that your soul prospers. There are countless areas of our soul where we need to prosper, or grow up. In this chapter, I want to focus primarily on two: God's instruction to give and the need to support your pastor.

Begin to Tithe

One of the fundamental principles of prosperity in Scripture is tithing. By definition, a *tithe* is one-tenth of something—in this case it is 10 percent of our earnings. The tithe is really the starting place that reveals our soul is beginning to prosper in the area of provision. God instructs us to...

> **MALACHI 3:10 *(NKJV)***
> **10 "Bring all the tithes into the storehouse, that there may be food in My house, and try Me now in this," says the Lord of hosts, "If I will not open for you the windows of heaven and pour out for you such blessing that there will not be room enough to receive it."**

What is the storehouse? It symbolically represents our local church, the place from where we are fed spiritually. In order for the gospel to continue to be preached, God desires and requires us to give back a portion of what He has given us. Again, the tithe is the starting place.

Some have argued, "Tithing is under the Law, and we are no longer under the Law. We are under grace." True, we are under the New Covenant of God's grace, but that does not nullify God's command to give. If anything, we should want to give more than the tithe because our new covenant with God is greater than the old one. Something else to keep in mind is that the principle of tithing was established through Abraham *before* the Law (see Genesis 14:18-20). Jesus gave His **all**. Shouldn't we want to give back to Him generously?

If a person's soul is prosperous, he will pay tithes of *all* his increase. I have discovered that if a person cannot tithe while earning $8 per hour, he will not tithe when earning $30 per hour. Why? Because his soul has not prospered to the place where he believes the tithe belongs to the Lord.

If someone babysits and she tithes from her $20 earnings, she is giving the same percentage as someone who tithes off a $10,000 increase. Yes, the $1,000 will help the church do a lot more, but from God's perspective, both individuals have given their portion. In some churches, there is an individual who makes such a large income that his tithe is more than everyone else's put together. Consequently, this person may think he is giving more than everyone else's share, but that is not true. He has only done what is required of him by the Word of God.

Some have thought that if their tithe is a huge amount, they should split it up and give it to different ministries. What chapter and verse of the Bible does that come from? Malachi 3 does *not* say to bring all the tithe into the storehous*es*. It also does not say to divide it up and bring it to your favorite ministries. It says to bring all the tithe into the storehouse, *singular*.

Some have said, "I like to feed the poor, and that's what I want to use my tithe for." Well, taking care of the poor is wonderful and commanded by God. But the money to do it is not supposed to come out of God's tithe. Feeding the poor falls under the category of "alms giving." These are freewill offerings we give in addition to our tithe. Your pastor and the leaders of your local church may designate a portion of the gifts received to care for those in need, but all your tithe should be brought into the storehouse. It is holy to the Lord (see Leviticus 27:30).

Your Tithe Helps Supply the Needs of God's House

As we learned in the last chapter, the primary purpose of prosperity is to establish God's covenant with people on the earth (see Deuteronomy 8:18). In New Testament terms, this means to finance the gospel, the New Covenant established through Jesus. This is where our tithe comes in. Financing the gospel provides the money needed to help people get saved and grow in Christ. It includes activities like supporting world missions, building churches, paying for television and radio time, producing teaching CDs and DVDs, printing books, buying advertising, and anything else necessary to get the message out.

The tithe also helps to pay for the seemingly insignificant and less dignified purchases, like running water, electricity, and supplies like toilet paper. Yes, I said toilet paper! If you only have two toilets in your church, this may not seem like a big deal. But can you imagine how much toilet paper a large ministry with dozens of toilets needs to buy? I know of one large church that has 110 toilets. Although expenses like these may seem unimportant, they are necessary to get the gospel out!

If we had a dozen orphan children lined up in front of our church with bloated bellies, we could probably raise enough money to pay off the building! A cause like this will always raise a lot of money because people are moved by their emotions when they see starving children. But when it comes to giving, we cannot be moved by our emotions more than we are moved by God's Word and His Spirit.

God says to bring all the tithe to the local church He has assigned you to, and we need to do it—no questions asked. All God requires of you is to be obedient and give. Remember His promise:

ISAIAH 1:19
19 If ye be willing and obedient, ye shall eat the good of the land:

Please understand, we need to help feed, clothe, and care for people in need. It is the heart of God. He says, "Pure and genuine religion in the sight of God the Father means caring for orphans and widows in their distress..." (James 1:27 NLT). At the same time, we must also give our tithe to provide for the basic operations of ministry. Both are important to advancing God's kingdom, and both yield rewards in this life and the one to come.

Provide for Your Pastor

When you give your tithe to your church, you are also providing for your pastor and all the staff that help the pastor. This too is a part of the purpose for prosperity. It is a God-ordained command—a command, unfortunately, that many believers are not aware of.

What did Jesus tell His disciples when He sent them out to announce the kingdom of God was at hand? He said,

> **MATTHEW 10:9-10** *(AMP)*
> **9 Take no gold nor silver nor [even] copper money in your purses (belts);**
> **10 And do not take a provision bag or a wallet for a collection bag for your journey, nor two undergarments, nor sandals, nor a staff; for the workman deserves his support (his living, his food).**

Notice that Jesus didn't instruct the twelve to save up their money so they would have provision to obey Him and preach the gospel. He also didn't encourage them to be bi-vocational ministers. He didn't say, "Bring your fishing poles along, boys! You're going to need them." None of that is in Scripture. As a matter of fact, when Peter went back to fishing in the last chapter of John, Jesus rebuked him! It's not because God is against work. But when He calls and separates a person to preach the gospel as a five-fold minister, He doesn't want him going back to his previous profession. I believe this is one of the reasons Jesus said,

> **LUKE 9:62** *(AMP)*
> **62 No one who puts his hand to the plow and looks back [to the things behind] is fit for the kingdom of God.**

Now don't misunderstand me. There may be times when a preacher will have to do secular work while getting started in the ministry, but it will only be for a season. If he tries to work a secular job when he should be working full-time in the ministry, he will "fish all night and catch *nothing*."

Providing for your pastor is also a major purpose for prosperity.

Here is my paraphrase of what Jesus said: "Go and preach that the kingdom of heaven is at hand, but when you go, don't bring any gold, silver, or copper in your money belts. And don't take any extra clothes. Leave them at home!" He didn't say this because the disciples had no money. They had money, otherwise Jesus wouldn't have said, "Don't bring your money belts." Jesus said this because He knew that wherever they would go, they would be provided for. He said, "The workman deserves his support."

Those who hear the message have been instructed to provide for the messenger. The people who are ministering to you should be taken care of by you. Period! God makes this very clear through the apostle Paul in 1

Corinthians 9:14. Carefully read through each version of this verse, paying close attention to the italicized words:

> **1 CORINTHIANS 9:14**
> 14 Even so hath the Lord ordained that they which preach the gospel *should live of the gospel.*
>
> **1 CORINTHIANS 9:14** *(AMP)*
> 14 [On the same principle] the Lord directed that those who publish the good news (the Gospel) *should live (get their maintenance) by the Gospel.*
>
> **1 CORINTHIANS 9:14** *(NLT)*
> 14 In the same way, the Lord ordered that those who preach the Good News *should be supported by those who benefit from it.*

Can you hear the Lord's heart? His will is that His ministers be abundantly provided for. Those who benefit from the good news being preached should be supporting those who preach it! This alleviates the pressure and stress from ministers having to provide for their own needs. It also enables them to focus their time and energy on teaching and equipping God's people—what they are called to do:

> **EPHESIANS 4:11-12** *(NLT)*
> 11 Now these are the gifts Christ gave to the church: the apostles, the prophets, the evangelists, and the pastors and teachers.
> 12 Their responsibility is to equip God's people to do his work and build up the church, the body of Christ.

Ministers are *gifts* to the church. They are extremely important and valuable. This is a godly mindset we must develop. What would happen if we had no ministers? The Bible says,

> **ROMANS 10:14-15**
> **14 How then shall they call on him in whom they have not believed? And how shall they believe in him of whom they have not heard? And how shall they hear without a preacher?**
> **15 And how shall they preach, except they be sent? As it is written, How beautiful are the feet of them that preach the gospel of peace, and bring glad tidings of good things!**

Preachers have to be sent by the Holy Spirit to preach the good news, and they need our financial backing to accomplish their call. Again, this is another valid purpose of prosperity.

Preachers Are More Important Than Buildings

Here is an absolute truth: Taking care of the pastor is more important than owning a building! I know of churches that have a beautiful building, but they don't adequately take care of their pastors. The Bible doesn't say, "For God so loved the world that He sent a *building*." It says He sent His *Son*. Jesus is the Good Shepherd who serves as the Chief Pastor over all His church. A building is just a tool. Pastors, teachers, evangelists, prophets, and apostles are gifts from Jesus. People are *always* more important than tools.

Religious, legalistic spirits often keep people from thinking correctly about preachers prospering. Sometimes people simply need to be taught this truth because it has never occurred to them. Think about it. When a couple plans their wedding, they seldom think about the blessing of having a pastor. The average wedding cost is about $28,400.[2] If people are shelling out this kind of money, does it seem right to pay the pastor $50? The flowers cost way more than that! And yet without a pastor, there would be no marriage ceremony.

In the Jewish faith, people understand the principle of providing for their ministers. Jews have never believed in poverty, and they take very good care of their rabbis. As of 2010, the average salary of a rabbi is $140,000 per year, and as a rule, they receive 1-2 percent of the total wedding budget to perform a wedding. The couple doesn't even blink about giving it. Sadly, according to a recent study conducted by The National Association of Church Business Administration, the average American pastor with a congregation of 300 people earns an annual salary of less than $28,000, and one out of five has to moonlight for supplemental income.[3] Folks, this needs to change!

Statistically, over 1,500 preachers leave the ministry every month.[4] And many Christian publications indicate that a high percentage of preachers' children drift away from the faith because they have seen how poorly their parents were treated by the church. Shouldn't we care for our pastors just as we would care for Jesus if He were pastoring us in the flesh? Yes! Most definitely!

His words, "If you do it unto the least of these, you have done it unto me," also applies to pastors.

Taking care of the pastor is more important than owning a building!

Studies have proven that churches that take good care of their pastors are healthier and far more blessed than churches that neglect their pastors. Buying groceries for your pastor may not seem very spiritual, but it is scriptural. Galatians 6:6 confirms this:

GALATIANS 6:6
6 Let him that is taught in the word communicate unto him that teacheth in all good things.

At face value, this verse in the King James Version seems to say, "Hey, give your pastor a nice card, thanking him for the truths he shares with you." But that is not what this verse is saying. A closer look at other translations makes it clear that God is instructing us to do more than give a verbal or written blessing. It is referring to a tangible, material blessing!

GALATIANS 6:6 *(Weymouth's)*
6 Let those who receive instruction in Christian truth *share with their instructors all temporal blessings*.

GALATIANS 6:6 *(AMP)*
6 Let him who receives instruction in the Word [of God] *share all good things with his teacher [contributing to his support]*.

Did you catch that? God wants us to share with our teachers and instructors a *tangible, material blessing*!

Many Christians feel good about giving financially to build a building or purchase equipment because these are accumulating assets. They figure that property appreciates with time, so it is a good investment. But without the pastor, there is no ministry. The pastor is the one who gives you God's messages that change your life, not the building or the high-tech sound equipment. Therefore, we can say that God's ministers are the greatest assets to the ministry! To support them is to support God Himself.

Remember what Jesus told His disciples before He sent them out:

> **MATTHEW 10:40 *(AMP)***
> **40 He who receives and welcomes and accepts you receives and welcomes and accepts Me, and he who receives and welcomes and accepts Me receives and welcomes and accepts Him Who sent Me.**

Honoring Your Pastor Releases Prosperity

Jesus made another interesting statement in His instruction to His disciples before He sent them out. He said,

> **MATTHEW 10:11**
> **11 And into whatsoever city or town ye shall enter, enquire who in it is worthy; and there abide till ye go thence.**

The word *enquire* in the Greek means to "examine or test thoroughly by questions; ascertain or interrogate." The word *worthy* means "deserving of a due reward."

The disciples were to look for a sincere, God-honoring person to stay with during their travels. They were to make sure (ascertain) that the family was peaceful, not fighting and bickering all the time, and that they had a reputation of integrity and generosity. They found this family through *enquiring*—searching and asking questions.

The household that took them in and provided for them was destined to receive a blessing. Those who provide for the preacher are deserving of a due reward. Jesus said,

MATTHEW 10:12-13
12 And when ye come into an house, salute it.
13 And if the house be worthy, let your peace come upon it: but if it be not worthy, let your peace return to you.

The word **peace** here is translated from a Greek word that actually implies "prosperity." So when someone took care of the preacher, the blessing of prosperity would come upon them and their household. God always rewards those who put His kingdom first!

What happened to those who rejected the preacher? Jesus said,

MATTHEW 10:14-15
14 And whosoever shall not receive you, nor hear your words, when ye depart out of that house or city, shake off the dust of your feet.
15 Verily I say unto you, it shall be more tolerable for the land of Sodom and Gomorrha in the day of judgment, than for that city.

If a city, church, or person does not receive the preacher and the message God sends, judgment will come to them. The disciples were instructed to shake the dust off their feet so that not even a little bit of that judgment would cling to them.

Those in the body of Christ who will not receive the preacher or the message he's been instructed to preach will someday face judgment. Withholding in the area of giving is the same as rejecting the message and the messenger, because giving allows the message to go forth. As believers, we really need to take these instructions from Christ seriously and obey them.

Renew Your Mind!

Don't let wrong thinking rob you, your pastor, and other fellow laborers from the prosperous life God desires. Renew your mind! Get rid of wrong thinking and replace it with right thinking found in God's Word. This is how to prosper your soul.

It really all comes down to spending time daily in God's Word and His presence. Scripture confirms this, instructing us to:

> **JAMES 1:21** *(AMP)*
> 21 Get rid of all uncleanness and the rampant outgrowth of wickedness, and in a humble (gentle, modest) spirit *receive and welcome the Word* which implanted and rooted [in your hearts] contains the power to *save your souls.*

I've said it before and I'll say it again, God's truth trumps tradition and all other erroneous thinking that goes against the knowledge of God. The only way we can discover His truth is by spending adequate time meditating on His Word.

There is more than enough money in this world. We have no need to fear running out of resources if we pay our tithe, give our offerings, and provide for our pastor. God will provide! He might not come through how or when we would expect, but He will come through. He is Jehovah Jireh—the Lord our Provider. He is also *El Shaddai*—the God who is more than enough! When He created this earth, He put more than enough resources in it to sustain all life. No need is too great for God to supply!

There will be times when you become fatigued and are tempted to stop giving. The devil will try to get you to quit by attacking you with difficulties. He doesn't want you to give your tithe or bless your pastor because he doesn't want God's kingdom to advance or either of you to prosper. Don't buy into his thinking! Don't quit! Keep doing the right thing. God says,

> **GALATIANS 6:9** *(NKJV)*
> 9 And let us not grow weary while doing good, for in due season we shall reap if we do not lose heart.

Support those who preach the gospel—do good every chance you get, working for the benefit of all. This is the primary purpose of prosperity. Understanding this truth will help prosper your soul so that the other areas of your life will prosper.

Remember, God has placed a built-in limiter for prosperity in you: He will only prosper you to the degree that your soul prospers. If you are not prospering, the solution is not working more hours or trying to make more money. The solution is to renew your mind with truth and allow your soul to prosper. In other words, get your soul in gear!

Chapter 8 Summary

Our prosperity from God is going to be in proportion to the prosperity, or spiritual health and maturity, of our soul. Two areas in which God wants our soul to mature are giving our tithe and offering and providing for our pastor. He wants us to give tangible, material blessings to those who minister to us. They represent Him. When we provide for God's ministers, we reap a reward—a reward of prosperity. Don't be moved by your emotions more than you are moved by God's Word and Spirit. Renew your mind with truth and get your soul in gear to prosper!

Chapter 9

Practical Principles of Prosperity

Now that you have discovered the truth that God wants you to prosper, you have to apply the Word of God to your life and expect it to work.

In this final chapter, we are going to look at ten practical principles that help produce prosperity. Some of these we have already discussed, but I want to mention them again here to help summarize our study. Although prosperity is part of your inheritance through Christ, these conditions must also be present in your life in order to experience the full, abundant life God has planned.

1. Prosperity Should *Not* Be Your Goal in Life.

A lot of people hear messages on prosperity and mistakenly think prosperity should be our goal, and that is simply not the case. Prosperity should *not* be your goal in life! **Your goal is to seek after God and live your life to please Him.**

God wants people in the New Testament times to prosper, just as He wanted people to prosper in the Old Testament times.

Our purpose for prosperity is not very different from those who lived before Abraham and from those who lived from Abraham until the resurrection of Jesus. Like them, our purpose is not just to live well and be comfortable. It is to glorify God, and in our case, this includes doing whatever it takes to preach the gospel to all the world. This often calls for sacrifice on our part.

Remember what the Bible teaches about Moses?

> **HEBREWS 11:24-26**
> **24 By faith Moses, when he was come to years, refused to be called the son of Pharaoh's daughter;**
> **25 Choosing rather to suffer affliction with the people of God, than to enjoy the pleasures of sin for a season;**
> **26 Esteeming the reproach of Christ greater riches than the treasures in Egypt: for he had respect unto the recompence of the reward.**

Moses chose to leave the wealth of Egypt and be counted as one of God's children. To him, this was a greater inheritance. If prosperity would have been Moses' number one goal, he would have never left the wealth of Egypt. As a result, he would have lost the priceless inheritance of walking in fellowship with God Himself and being one of the greatest history makers the world has ever known.

My point is that **our commitment to the Lord has to be number one!** Prosperity is not number two or even number three. Prosperity is the byproduct of putting God first and obediently carrying out our God-given call. Indeed, when seeking the Lord is our way of life, we are in position to truly prosper.

2. Seek the Lord.

If you want to prosper on every level, you have to *seek the Lord*. When I say seek the Lord, I am not saying to seek Him just so that He will prosper you. That is the wrong motive, and wrong motives will always hinder prosperity. God wants you to seek Him for fellowship. He is jealous for your love and attention and yearns to hold first place in your life (see James 4:5).

Uzziah was sixteen years old when he became king over Judah. To his credit, he did something many other political leaders fail to do—he sought the Lord! The Scripture says,

> **2 CHRONICLES 26:1-5**
> **1 Then all the people of Judah took Uzziah, who was sixteen years old, and made him king in the room of his father Amaziah.**
> **2 He built Eloth, and restored it to Judah, after that the king slept with his fathers.**
> **3 Sixteen years old was Uzziah when he began to reign, and he reigned fifty and two years in Jerusalem. His mother's name also was Jecoliah of Jerusalem.**
> **4 And he did that which was right in the sight of the Lord, according to all that his father Amaziah did.**

> 5 And *he sought God* in the days of Zechariah, who had understanding in the visions of God: and *as long as he sought the Lord, God made him to prosper.*

Uzziah didn't trust in his own understanding, but acknowledged God in all his ways. He sought the Lord, and as a result, God made him prosper! Seeking the Lord *first* is a condition for every Christian as well. When you seek the Lord, He will show you things, and when you are obedient to do what he shows you, you will prosper! Jesus said,

> **MATTHEW 6:33**
> 33 But seek ye first the kingdom of God, and his righteousness; and all these things shall be added unto you.

Think of all the people you know. There are probably hundreds. How many of those hundreds do you think are *seeking first the kingdom of God*? How about you? If someone was to casually observe your life, would they be able to say that of you? Many people cry, "Lord, I need this thing and that thing added to me!" But they don't receive it because their motive is wrong—their focus is on the gift, not the giver.

The key to having our needs met is to seek first the kingdom of God—to make His way of "doing and being right" top priority. It's putting His business ahead of our business. When we live like this, all that we have need of will be provided.

The key to having our needs met is to seek first the kingdom of God, putting His business ahead of our business.

3. Renew Your Mind.

A third condition that leads to prosperity is the renewing of our mind with truth. As we learned earlier, this is not a one-time event but an ongoing lifestyle. Renewing our mind is not a suggestion; it is a command. God clearly instructs us through the apostle Paul,

> **ROMANS 12:2** *(NKJV)*
> **2 Do not be conformed to this world, but be transformed by the *renewing of your mind*, that you may prove what *is* that good and acceptable and perfect will of God.**

At any given time, one of two things is happening: You are either being *conformed* to the customs, culture, and thinking of this world, or you are being *transformed* into the image of Christ. It's easy to conform to the ways of the world. All you have to do is *nothing*. But to be transformed into the image of Christ requires effort—it means you regularly feed on the Word of God and allow the Holy Spirit to make His thoughts your thoughts.

When I first became a Christian, I was not aware that God wanted me to prosper. I don't remember any preacher talking about the principles of tithing and giving offerings. Nor do I remember hearing about the purpose for prosperity. Nevertheless, there were people who attended my church who were very prosperous—some even drove Mercedes. When I saw that, I remember thinking, *Would Jesus drive a Mercedes? Wouldn't He drive a Chevy? That seems more appropriate.*

This kind of thinking is common among Christians who have unrenewed minds. In essence, I, like many others, believed it was spiritual to be poor. This mindset is a tactic of the enemy that keeps a lot of Christians living outside of the abundant life provided through Christ.

The truth is no one really wants to be poor. Success and prosperity are etched in our hearts, and I was no exception. Although I didn't understand prosperity, I did understand the importance of seeking the Lord. Within a short time, I was exposed to right teaching, and my mind began to be renewed with truth, such as the foundational truth found in 3 John 2:

3 JOHN 2
2 Beloved, I wish above all things that thou mayest prosper and be in health, even as thy soul prospereth.

As we learned earlier, our soul is our mind, will, and emotions. In order to prosper in life, you have to prosper your soul. Notice I said *you* have to do it. How do you prosper your soul? You do it by feeding on the Word of God and renewing your mind to think the way God thinks. God is not limited in any way. His power is immeasurable, His resources inexhaustible! Scripture says He...

EPHESIANS 3:20 (*NKJV*)
20 ...Is able to do exceedingly abundantly above all that we ask or think, according to the power that works in us.

As Christians, we need to think bigger! We need to realize that money is *not* a big deal to God. Think about a movie star who earns $20 million to make one movie.

In one day, some stars earn $100,000. In ten days, they would earn $1 million. Working 200 days at $100,000 a day would yield them $20 million. How much is that an hour? Well, if we estimate that our star works 10 hours a day for 100 days, earning $20 million, that would amount to $2,000 per hour.

Does this stretch your thinking a bit? I hope so. And that's only a dab of all the wealth that is in the world. To some people, $20 million is chump change! This includes God. "Well, that's not what normal people earn," you may say. We have to stop thinking like "normal" people and start thinking like God's people! Getting the gospel out is a big job that takes big bucks. God will get it *to* you if He knows He can get it *through* you.

God can give large amounts of money to people whom He can trust because He knows they'll be faithful with it. Some people vow, "If I had a lot of money, I'd give a lot of it to God's work." But would they really? Jesus addressed this saying,

> **LUKE 16:10 *(NKJV)***
> **10 He who is faithful in what is least is faithful also in much; and he who is unjust in what is least is unjust also in much.**

Many people cannot handle a lot of money because of wrong thinking. As I said before, those who win the lottery often end up losing all of their winnings and ruining their lives because they don't know how to handle money. It's not because money is evil. It's the *love of* money that is the root of all evil (see 1 Timothy 6:10).

So don't let wrong thinking limit your ability to prosper. Renew your mind!

> **EPHESIANS 4:22-24** *(AMP)*
> 22 Strip yourselves of your former nature [put off and discard your old unrenewed self] which characterized your previous manner of life and becomes corrupt through lusts and desires that spring from delusion;
> 23 And *be constantly renewed in the spirit of your mind* [having a fresh mental and spiritual attitude],
> 24 And put on the new nature (the regenerate self) created in God's image, [Godlike] in true righteousness.

4. Pay Your Tithes and Be a Giver.

The Bible teaches us to be givers. Giving is the nature of God, and He wants us to follow His example (see Ephesians 5:1).

What you do with what you get determines how much more you get. If you spend all your income on yourself, you will not prosper. You can pray, confess God's promises on prosperity, and work three jobs, but it won't do you any good if you are not obeying God's Word to give.

Remember, the tithe is the starting point when it comes to giving financially. It is the first ten percent of all your increase, and it belongs to God. He instructs us to...

> **MALACHI 3:10**
> 10 Bring ye ALL the tithes into the storehouse...

The tithe is God's, and it must be set apart as holy. He is the One who gives us the power to succeed and get wealth, not us (see Deuteronomy 8:18). If I take your Bible and say to you, "I have a gift for you, and you are really going to like it. As a matter of fact, it has your name written on it," and then I give you your own Bible, I really haven't given you anything. It was yours to begin with. Likewise, when we pay our tithes, we are simply giving God what is already His. Only after you have paid your tithes are you able to give an offering, because an offering is above and beyond the tithe.

The Lord wants us to imitate Him and be givers. This applies not only to money, but also our time, talent, attention, love, kindness, and respect. The list of what we can give is endless. Jesus said,

LUKE 6:38
38 Give, and it shall be given unto you; good measure, pressed down, and shaken together, and running over, shall men give into your bosom. For with the same measure that ye mete withal it shall be measured to you again.

Does this mean that if you don't give, it won't be given unto you? That's correct. God multiplies what we give. If we give away zero (nothing), than zero times anything always equals zero. You have to give something before He can multiply it! And I believe this is referring to offerings, not the tithe. The tithe is something we *pay*, and an offering is something we *give*.

I read a story about a preacher who came home one day and there was a brand new Mercedes in his driveway. Someone had given it to him as a gift. A few days later he came home and there was another new Mercedes in his driveway for his wife. You may be thinking, *Man it would be nice to come home and find a brand new Mercedes in my driveway,* and I agree. But it's important to note that this same preacher had given away fourteen vehicles prior to receiving the two new Mercedes. How many Christians do you know who have given away that many cars?

Now don't get me wrong. Giving away a car in order to get a car is not a magic formula or a proper motive. The key is being willing and *obedient*. Obeying what God's Holy Spirit is leading us to do throughout our daily lives is what opens the door to a harvest of blessing. The Lord may or may not ask you to give a car away. Actually, unless He tells you to give your car away, I don't recommend doing it. If you do, you may end up walking for a season.

Again, God's promise is,

ISAIAH 1:19
19 If ye be *willing* **and** *obedient***, ye shall eat the good of the land.**

God desires to lead and instruct all believers in the best way to live. But to those who have not obeyed Him in what He has instructed, He doesn't give additional instructions. They must humble themselves, ask for His forgiveness, and then do what He has asked.

I saw a comic strip once that showed a man being water baptized. As he was going under the water, he held his wallet up in the air so that it wouldn't go under with him. What a true depiction this is for many. Jesus gave His all for us, but have we been willing to give our all for Him? Many have reasoned that they simply cannot afford to pay their tithes. What they fail to realize is that 100% of their income *without* the blessing of God on it will be far less than 90% of their income *with* the blessing on it! The devil will see to it that your money gets devoured by extra needs when you're not a tither.

I encourage you to surrender all that you are and all that you have to God. Refuse to be too attached to anything and be willing to give away anything that He prompts you to give. This is the way to get into the supernatural flow of God's abundance! The Scripture says,

GALATIANS 6:7
7 Be not deceived; God is not mocked: for whatsoever a man soweth, that shall he also reap.

I also like the Phillips translation of this verse. It says,

GALATIANS 6:7 (*Phillips*)
7 ...A man's harvest in life will depend entirely on what he SOWS!

Here's a wild thought: Why not make a commitment to sow some kind of seed every day for the next 30 days into other people's lives? It can be a financial seed, like buying someone a cup of coffee, or a material possession, like giving away a favorite tie or shirt. You may want to keep a journal of all the things you give as well as all the things you receive. I believe as you "Cast your bread upon the waters...you will find it after many days" (Ecclesiastes 11:1 AMP).

5. Make a Budget and Plan Your Spending.

It is scriptural to keep a good record of the money you have coming in (income) and how it is being spent (expenditures). People who spend more money than they earn will eventually run into serious problems. I believe this is the heart behind God's instruction in Proverbs 27:23-24:

> **PROVERBS 27:23-24 *(AMP)***
> **23 Be diligent to know the state of your flocks, and look well to your herds;**
> **24 For riches are not forever....**

In Old Testament times, flocks and herds were like liquid assets used to buy and sell. "Knowing the state of your flocks" meant to have a handle on your financial status. For us today, this means having a budget.

In simplest terms, a budget is an itemized overview of reoccurring expenses, like your house note and electric bill, and projected expenses, like food and fuel. A good budget serves as a financial road map that takes you from where you are to where you want to be each month. It helps you specifically see where your money is going.

Now, if you ask the average person if he has a budget, he will say yes and rattle off the big items he spends his money on. However, he is often unable to accurately track where the rest of his money goes. With the help of the Holy Spirit, you can learn how to live within the margin of what you earn, developing a healthy balance between *spending* some, *saving* some, and *giving* some.

From my experience as a pastor for over 28 years, I have found that about 90 percent of all Christians don't know how to handle money. More often than not, the problem is linked to two root issues: They are not tithing or they have not developed a budget to follow.[5]

Even wealthy people use budgets, and as crazy as it sounds, even people involved in illegal activity use them. They usually have two sets of books. One set is for their accountant and the IRS, and the other is for them to track the illegal activity they don't want anyone to know about.

If you don't have a budget, it's time to develop one. "But having a budget scares me," you may say. "What if I can't stick to it? What if I spend more than I allotted in some areas?" It's alright. Don't be afraid. Developing a budget and learning to follow it will take time. Costs will change as your family grows and the economy shifts, so take the liberty to tweak your plan as needed.

One thing's for sure: If you fail to plan, you plan to fail. Don't wait for the "perfect time" to make a budget. Scripture says, "If you wait for perfect conditions, you will never get anything done" (Ecclesiastes 11:4 TLB). Take time to prayerfully develop a monthly budget of spending, saving, and giving. God will bless the plan that He directs you to create.

6. Count the Cost.

Of all the topics Jesus taught on, money was one of the most frequent. From the parable of the lost coin to the parable of the talents, He was never at a loss for words when it came to financial matters. On one occasion, He emphasized the importance of *counting the cost* before taking on something new. He said,

> **LUKE 14:28-30**
> **28 For which of you, intending to build a tower, sitteth not down first, and *counteth the cost*, whether he have sufficient to finish it?**
> **29 Lest haply, after he hath laid the foundation, and is not able to finish it, all that behold it begin to mock him,**
> **30 Saying, This man began to build, and was not able to finish.**

Each new endeavor you are considering should be carefully calculated to determine how much time, money, and effort will be required to complete it. Some things will need hours of planning. Others will require days, weeks, and even months. The greater the venture, the more planning it will entail.

Years ago, our church seriously considered opening a Christian bookstore in a storefront. Prior to this, we had managed a number of book and resource tables at our church and had been successful at it. But overseeing a book table and running a bookstore in a storefront are two very different things.

Thank God I didn't have an arrogant attitude, thinking I knew all about bookstores. Instead, I humbled myself and went to some people I knew who owned and operated bookstores and began asking a lot of questions. I also spoke to some distributors and researched all the fixtures we would need. After much prayer, exploration, and carefully calculating the cost, we concluded that opening a bookstore was not a good idea at that time.

Before you plan to start a business or launch out in ministry, pray for direction! This is the first step. In addition to prayer and being led by the Holy Spirit, *do your homework!* **Count the cost** of what it is going to take to make your idea become a reality. If you reach the conclusion that it won't work out, don't step out. You should not proceed unless you have very *clear* direction from the Lord.

Someone may say, "But you just wasted a lot of time!" No, you just saved your hide! People who don't take the time to count the cost are destined for difficulty. Some people don't want to figure anything out. They just jump right into business endeavors or purchases without any research or prayer, only to regret it later when they run into financial trouble. God's Word is clear:

PROVERBS 19:2 *(NLT)*
2 **Enthusiasm without knowledge is no good; haste makes mistakes.**

Not counting the cost is a sure way to go broke. Don't ever be too proud to talk to others who know more than you. If you haven't had previous experience with the type of business or ministry you are considering, I strongly suggest you go and work for someone in that same field for a year or two and learn all that you can.

Then if you still plan to open your own place, don't buy all new equipment until you get enough business to justify it. Give your new endeavor at least a year of operation to see how things turn out before going into unnecessary debt.

What does all this have to do with prosperity? A lot! It's called **planning**. Don't let enthusiasm rule over wisdom. When you make plans, make sure you seek and secure the wisdom of God just as King Uzziah did. Wisdom comes from spending time in His Word, sitting in His presence, and listening for the voice of His Spirit. Scripture says,

> **PROVERBS 3:13-16**
> **13 Happy is the man that findeth wisdom, and the man that getteth understanding.**
> **14 For the merchandise of it is better than the merchandise of silver, and the gain thereof than fine gold.**
> **15 She is more precious than rubies: and all the things thou canst desire are not to be compared unto her.**
> **16 Length of days is in her right hand; and in her left hand riches and honour.**

7. Don't Be Lazy.

Did you know that one of the sins of the people of Sodom was *laziness*? You can check it out for yourself in Ezekiel 16:49. The Bible has a lot to say about laziness, and none of it is good.

PROVERBS 18:9 *(NLT)*
9 A lazy person is as bad as someone who destroys things.
Proverbs 15:19 *(NKJV)*
19 Laziness casts one into a deep sleep, and an idle person will suffer hunger.
ECCLESIASTES 10:18 *(NLT)*
18 Laziness leads to a sagging roof; idleness leads to a leaky house.

One of my mentors, used to say, "God doesn't bless stingy people or lazy people," and it's true. He wants us to work and to be diligent about what He has called us to do. Through the writer of Hebrews, He says,

HEBREWS 6:11-12 *(NKJV)*
11 And we desire that each one of you show the same diligence to the full assurance of hope until the end,
12 That you do not become sluggish, but imitate those who through faith and patience inherit the promises.

Some people think that because they are making minimum wage, they don't have to work very hard. They say, "If it was my own business, then I'd put my all into it." But that is what I call stinking-thinking—it is a worldly, sinful, and selfish attitude! People like this will always work for someone else and wonder why they never get ahead. Jesus Himself said,

LUKE 16:12 *(NKJV)*
12 And if you have not been faithful in what is another man's, who will give you what is your own?

A few others scriptures help drive this point home:

ROMANS 12:11 *(NLT)*
11 Never be lazy, but work hard and serve the Lord enthusiastically.

PROVERBS 13:4 *(NLT)*
4 Lazy people want much but get little, but those who work hard will prosper.

8. Don't Be Impulsive!

The old adage, "Haste makes waste," is accurate and a good warning to heed. Impulsive choices are made in a hurry and almost always get us into trouble. Remember Esau? He impulsively chose a bowl of stew in exchange for his first-born birthright—a choice he regretted for the rest of his life (see Genesis 25:29-33). Make no mistake:

PROVERBS 21:5 *(The Message)*
5 Careful planning puts you ahead in the long run; hurry and scurry puts you further behind.

I have found that by simply waiting and praying about things, God has saved me a ton of money. Often times, a repairman will diagnose a problem with something in my house or with my car, and the estimate to fix it will be very high. If I don't have to deal with it right away, I have learned to wait and pray about what I should do. After a little more research and being led to the right people, the repairs have often ended up being something simple that didn't require the total estimated cost.

An eager repairman or salesman can talk you into buying many unnecessary things if you don't take time to hear from God. Be especially sensitive to what His Spirit is speaking to your spirit before making expensive purchases like houses, cars, and appliances. Be sure you are buying the right thing, at the right time, for the right price. If you are a person who is tempted to do things quickly, learn not to give in to the impulses of your flesh.

How can you tell if you are impulsive? If you frequently make unplanned purchases, especially items located in the checkout lane at the store, it is a good indication. Impulse buying is a multi-billion dollar industry. If you buy everything you see, you're going to be broke while making someone else rich. You can't buy everything your beady little eyes see! There is a time and a place for everything.

You can't buy everything your beady little eyes see or you'll go broke!

---

9. Beware of Extravagance and Excess.

Excess is the enemy's playground. If he can get us *out of balance* and into extravagance in any area of our lives, he has gained a foothold of control in our soul. And a foothold is just a few steps away from a stronghold. This is why the Lord instructs us to...

1 PETER 5:8 *(AMP)*
8 ***Be well balanced*** **(temperate, sober of mind), be vigilant and cautious at all times; for that enemy of yours, the devil, roams around like a lion roaring [in fierce hunger], seeking someone to seize upon and devour.**

A person who does *not* have the money to live extravagantly, but spends his money as though he does, will not prosper. If you receive an extravagant gift by faith, then it is not excessive. If you live extravagantly but are obediently paying your tithe and giving generously as the Lord leads, then you are not in excess.

What does unhealthy extravagance look like? Imagine a church buying a $5,000 microphone, but they only have $100 Radio Shack speakers. This would be extravagant and downright foolish. The microphone may be great, but it will never produce the high-quality sound it is capable of through $100 speakers.

Here's another example I have seen. Picture a person living in a run-down neighborhood who is paying a mortgage on a $30,000 home and also has a $50,000 to $100,000 car in his driveway. This is out of balance.

Keep in mind that what may be excessive for one person may not be excessive for another. It all depends on personal circumstances and how the Lord is leading each individual. At this point in my ministry, a personal jet would be extravagant. But for someone who travels every week to minister, it would not be. It would be helpful.

Stop and take an honest inventory of your life. Ask yourself, *Am I living a balanced life, or have I crossed the line into excess and extravagance?* Pray and ask the Lord for His insight. He sees things clearly and will give you His eyes to see what needs to change and the power and plan to make it happen!

10. Always Allow Facts and Faith to Work Together.

We have to learn not to spend every bit of increase we receive. It is wise to regularly set aside money for another day or purpose. It's also good to pray and ask the Lord if He has a purpose for the increase He has allowed you to receive.

For example, let's say you get a $100-a-week raise. You could rejoice and immediately decide to go out and purchase a new car that requires a $400 monthly payment. The only problem is you haven't counted the cost or done proper planning. Once taxes are taken out and you pay your tithe and possibly give an offering, there won't be $400 left for a car payment. You will probably only have about $250-280. So committing to a $400 monthly car payment would actually put you in a financial hole $120-150 each month. This type of money management will keep you from prospering.

Many people in a situation like this realize in their spirit they should not buy that extra item, but because their desires and emotions are driving them, they push past what they know and get it anyway. Unless we have the witness of the Spirit—His internal peace and approval—we should not spend money outside of our financial margins. Even a person who is in faith should make calculations because he needs to know what to believe for. You do not want to step out in faith for something unless you KNOW exactly what you're believing for.

Every year when I am praying about how much income we should believe for—for our church and personally—I run the numbers several different ways and make realistic projections. Once I see what the facts are, I pray and ask the Lord what I should believe for. I don't make a decision based on the facts alone. The facts help me locate where my faith is, and then the two are able to work together to guide my decisions. The same will hold true for you.

I know a preacher who was warned by the Lord of a coming recession. To navigate through the tough times ahead, God instructed him to let seventeen people go. I know it sounds harsh, but I'm sure the Lord had other jobs for them—possibly better jobs. If this preacher wanted to do well financially during the recession, he had to obey the Lord.

Some might think, *Well, why didn't he just use his faith to keep them on the payroll? Why didn't he just stand on Philippians 4:19?* To that I say, once you have heard the word of the Lord, you can no longer have faith for anything different than that word. You cannot use one word (Scripture) to negate another word. Faith does not work that way. By faith, this preacher obeyed the Lord and was saved from financial trouble. When a person is led by the Holy Spirit, he will learn to manage what he has and not be in lack.

If you are considering starting your own business, first be sure that the Spirit is leading you. Realize that just because you have great skill doesn't mean you have great business sense. You may be the best auto repairman in the shop you work for, but if you know nothing about the business operations, it would be foolish to try to open your own shop until you learn them.

There are great athletes and famous actors who make millions of dollars, yet some of them end up in financial trouble because they are poor money managers. How can a person who makes millions upon millions of dollars end up in big financial trouble? It could be poor management, lust, greed, or just plain stupidity.

Remember, any business endeavor requires homework and proper management. Always allow the facts you discover to work together with your faith, not independently. Seek God first for direction and confirmation of what He is asking you to do. Get quiet in His presence—pray, fast, and listen for His guidance. He will never ask you to do anything that is contradictory to His Word. His path for your life will always be marked by peace!

Are You in Financial Trouble? Don't Panic...God Has a Plan!

If you are experiencing financial trouble, don't panic and don't be discouraged. God has a plan! He says in His Word,

JEREMIAH 29:11 *(AMP)*
11 For I know the thoughts and plans that I have for you, says the Lord, thoughts and plans for welfare and peace and not for evil, to give you hope in your final outcome.

If you are in financial trouble, you will have to find ways to cut costs. This is not usually easy, but it is doable with God's help. Although taking a few steps back may feel like you are going in reverse, it doesn't necessarily mean you are not making progress. If you fall into a ditch while climbing a mountain, you have to get out of the ditch before you can start climbing again!

Years ago when I was in Bible school, my car's transmission broke, and it would only drive in reverse. The car had been having problems for a while, but I didn't have the money to repair it. When it finally got to the point where it would only go in reverse, I couldn't just leave it on the side of the road. It would have been towed away, creating not only a towing bill but also a storage fee for each day it sat in the tow yard.

What did I do? I drove my car *backward* all the way to my apartment! Going backward in that situation actually put me ahead financially. The same may be true for you. Cutting back may seem like you are going backward, but it will actually put you ahead financially in the long run. Where you are now is not where you will be forever. You may have to do without a number of amenities you have grown accustomed to, but if you're following God's plan for your life it will only be for a season. Just as the Holy Spirit empowered Jesus to endure, He will empower you!

Jesus was able to endure the cross because He was focused on something far greater on the other side of it—the joy of restored relationship with you and me. God wants us…

HEBREWS 12:2
2 Looking unto Jesus the author and finisher of our faith; who for the joy that was set before him endured the cross, despising the shame, and is set down at the right hand of the throne of God.

If you keep your eyes on the prize of intimately knowing Christ, everything else will fall into place. The Holy Spirit will empower you to get ahead financially and stick with a plan for getting out of debt. Keep in mind that your goal in life is **not** financial abundance. Your goal is to *be a blessing*—to use what God has given you to get the gospel out and make disciples of all nations. This is the primary purpose for prosperity.

Don't ever let going after wealth be your priority. Seek the Lord! Ask Him to give you His view of prosperity, and He will. Ask Him to liberate you from wrong thinking and renew your mind. Get wisdom and understanding by spending time in His Word and His presence. Remember, Abraham's blessings are your blessings through Jesus! Claim them as you seek to prosper your soul. By God's grace, He will take you from faith to faith and from one level of glory to the next. ***No matter what your situation is, God is bigger!*** Trust Him, and Thou Shalt Not Lack!

Chapter 9 Summary

Prosperity should not be your goal in life. Your goal is to seek the Lord and live your life to please Him. As you put His business ahead of your business, your needs will be met. As you seek Him and spend time in His Word, your mind will be renewed and your thinking expanded. What you do with what you get determines how much more you get, so live to give. Obey what God's Spirit is leading you to do in your daily life, and you'll open the door to a harvest of blessing. Remember to make a good budget and follow it. Count the cost before taking on any new endeavor, and don't be lazy! Work hard at what God has called you to do. Don't be impulsive or live in excess; don't spend every bit of increase you receive. Save some for another day and purpose. Always allow the facts and your faith to work together to guide your decisions. **No matter what your situation is, God is bigger! Trust Him, and Thou Shalt Not Lack!**

Endnotes

[1] "Odds of Winning the Lottery". http://www.savingadvice.com/forums/other/5559-probability-winning-lottery-dont-waste-your-money.html, retrieved 4/10/13.

[2] "Average Wedding Bill in 2012: $28,400". http://money.cnn.com/2013/03/10/pf/wedding-cost/index.html, retrieved 4/30/13.

[3] "A Pastor's Salary". Crown Financial Ministries. http://www.crown.org/library/viewarticle.aspx?articleid=148, retrieved 5/17/13.

[4] "Statistics on Pastors". 2007 (research from 1989 to 2006). Krejcir, R. J., Ph.D. Francis A. Schaeffer Institute of Church Leadership Development. http://www.intothyword.org/apps/articles/default.asp?articleid=36562&columnid=3958.

[5] "Study: Few Born Agains Tithe to Churches". Barrick, Audrey. The Christian Post. April 14, 2008. http://m.christianpost.com/news/study-few-born-agains-tithe-to-churches-31947/

A Prayer to Receive Jesus As Your Savior

"Heavenly Father, I come to You right now in the name of Jesus. Your Word says, '*...him that cometh to Me I will in no wise cast out*' (John 6:37), so I know You won't cast me out. You will take me in, and I thank You for it.

You said in Your Word, '*...If thou shalt confess with thy mouth the Lord Jesus, and shalt believe in thine heart that God hath raised Him from the dead, thou shalt be saved...For whosoever shall call upon the name of the Lord shall be saved*' (Romans 10:9, 13).

I believe in my heart that Jesus Christ is the Son of God. I believe He died for my sins and was raised from the dead so that I could be in right standing with You. I am calling upon His Name, the name of Jesus, so I know that You are saving me right now.

Your Word says, '*...with the HEART man believeth unto righteousness; and with the MOUTH confession is made unto salvation*' (Romans 10:10). I believe with my heart, and confess with my mouth that Jesus is my Lord. Therefore, I am now saved! Thank You, Father. In Jesus name, Amen!"

About the Author

Jeff Miller is a bold, inspirational teacher of the Word of God. His simple and often humorous style helps bring clarity to timeless, biblical truths. Jeff was born-again at the age of seventeen through an unusual and spectacular visitation from the Lord. Since that day in January of 1975, he has ministered in Bible studies, Bible schools, churches, conferences, and has preached the gospel in many nations of the world, including India, Russia, the Philippines, Thailand, Peru, Costa Rica, and Mexico.

Pastor Jeff is a 1979 graduate of New Life Bible College and a 1982 graduate of Rhema Bible Training Center. He is ordained under Ed Dufresne Ministries and Rhema Ministerial Association Int'l. Jeff has been in full-time ministry for over thirty years and has pioneered two churches, including Abundant Life Family Church in Aurora, Illinois, where he currently serves as senior pastor. He and his wife, Christine, have been married for over twenty-eight years and have three children—Elizabeth, Timothy, and Kaitlin.

For additional copies of this book,
other teaching materials by Jeff and Christine Miller,
or to schedule a time of ministry at your church,
please contact:

P.O. Box 6404, Aurora, IL 60598
630.851.LIFE
PastorsJeffandChristine.org

The book is also available as an eBook
through major distributors.
Go online and share this book/message today!

www.ingramcontent.com/pod-product-compliance
Lightning Source LLC
LaVergne TN
LVHW051557080426
835510LV00020B/3020

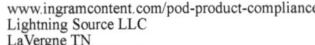